MODERN AFRICAN
POLITICAL LEADERS

Also by R. Kent Rasmussen

Mzilikazi of the Ndebele
Migrant Kingdom: Mzilikazi's Ndebele in South Africa
Dictionary of African Historical Biography
Historical Dictionary of Rhodesia/Zimbabwe
Historical Dictionary of Zimbabwe
*Mark Twain A to Z: The Essential Reference to His Life and
    Writings*
Mark Twain's Book for Bad Boys and Girls
Farewell to Jim Crow: The Rise and Fall of Segregation in America
*The Quotable Mark Twain: His Essential Aphorisms, Witticisms
    and Concise Opinions*

GL⬤BAL PROFILES

MODERN AFRICAN POLITICAL LEADERS

R. Kent Rasmussen

☑ Facts On File, Inc.

Modern African Political Leaders
Copyright © 1998 by R. Kent Rasmussen

Facts On File, Inc.
11 Penn Plaza
New York NY 10001

Library of Congress Cataloging-in-Publication Data

Rasmussen, R. Kent.
    Modern African political leaders / R. Kent Rasmussen.
        p. cm.—(Global profiles)
    Includes bibliographical references and index.
    Summary: Profiles eight modern African political leaders,
including Nelson Mandela and Haile Selassie.
    ISBN 0-8160-3277-7 (alk. paper)
    1. Heads of state—Africa—Biography—Juvenile literature.
    2. Statesmen—Africa—Biography—Juvenile literature. 3. Africa—Politics and government—1945–1960—Juvenile literature.
    4. Africa—Politics and government—1960–   —Juvenile literature.
    [1. Heads of state—Africa. 2. Statesmen—Africa. 3. Africa—
Politics and government—1945–1960. 4. Africa—Politics and
government—1960–   ] I. Title. II. Series.
    DT36.R37 1998
    960.3'2'0922—dc 21
    [B]   97-31162

Facts On File books are available at special discounts when purchased in bulk quantities for businesses, associations, institutions, or sales promotions. Please call our Special Sales Department in New York at (212) 967-8800 or (800) 322-8755.

You can find Facts On File on the World Wide Web at http://www.factsonfile.com

Text design by Cathy Rincon
Cover design by Nora Wertz
Illustration on page viii by Dale Williams

Printed in the United States of America

MP FOF 10 9 8 7 6 5 4 3 2 1

This book is printed on acid-free paper.

To Jim Armstrong

Africanist, bibliophile, and friend

Contents

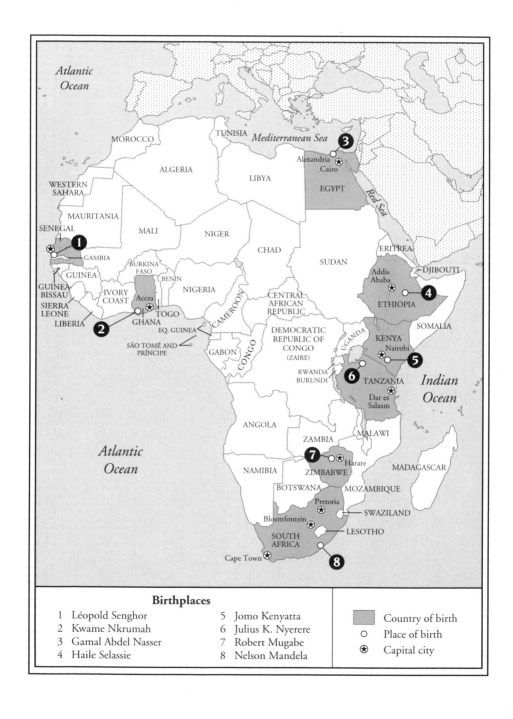

Atlantic
Ocean

MOROCCO

TUNISIA   *Mediterranean Sea*   ❸

ALGERIA   LIBYA   Alexandria○ ✴
                                     Cairo

WESTERN
SAHARA   EGYPT
                                              Red Sea
MAURITANIA

SENEGAL   ERITREA
         ❶   MALI   NIGER
                                                    ⤙DJIBOUTI
     GAMBIA   CHAD   SUDAN   Addis
                                                   Ababa
GUINEA   BURKINA   ✴   ❹
         FASO
GUINEA-   BENIN   ETHIOPIA
BISSAU IVORY   NIGERIA   SOMALIA
SIERRA COAST Accra
LEONE   ○   CAMEROON CENTRAL   KENYA
LIBERIA   ❷   TOGO   AFRICAN   Nairobi
              GHANA   REPUBLIC   UGANDA ○ ✴
                   EQ. GUINEA   ❺
         SÃO TOMÉ AND ⤙   DEMOCRATIC
         PRÍNCIPE   REPUBLIC OF
                   GABON   CONGO   RWANDA
                       CONGO (ZAIRE)   BURUNDI ❻   TANZANIA   *Indian*
                                                                Ocean
                                                  Dar es
                                                  Salaam ✴
                                ANGOLA
                                        ZAMBIA   MALAWI
Atlantic   MADAGASCAR
Ocean   NAMIBIA ❼ ○Harare
                                         ZIMBABWE   MOZAMBIQUE
                                 BOTSWANA
                                       Pretoria ✴   SWAZILAND
                                 Bloemfontein○✴
                                               ⤙LESOTHO
                                       SOUTH
                                       AFRICA
                            Cape Town○✴ ❽

Birthplaces

1 Léopold Senghor	5 Jomo Kenyatta	▦ Country of birth
2 Kwame Nkrumah	6 Julius K. Nyerere	○ Place of birth
3 Gamal Abdel Nasser	7 Robert Mugabe	✴ Capital city
4 Haile Selassie	8 Nelson Mandela	

Introduction

Africa is a remarkable continent for many reasons. Of these, perhaps the most remarkable is the extraordinary profusion of political changes that have taken place there since midcentury. With the possible exception of post-Soviet Eastern Europe, no other part of the world has seen so much political change in so short a time.

When the United Nations formed in 1945 its total membership comprised only 51 nations, including four from Africa. Five decades later its membership included 53 nations from Africa alone. The fact that Africa accounted for nearly 30 percent of the total U.N. membership in 1995 was extraordinary. Even more extraordinary, perhaps, was the fact that all but four of these 53 African nations came into existence *after* the United Nations was created. Any study of modern African political leadership is, therefore, a study of change. The profiles contained in this volume are filled with stories of dramatic and often surprising developments—many without parallel in Western political history.

At midcentury most African countries were still under European colonial rule. Moreover, some of those that were independent were not quite as independent as they might have appeared. One of these, Liberia, a tiny West African country ruled by descendants of freed American slaves, had been an independent republic for a century. In many ways, however, it remained a client state of the United States. Egypt had been formally independent since 1922, but its people still rankled at a lingering British presence that more than once had made a mockery of Egyptian sovereignty. An exception was the Union of South Africa. Created in 1910, it gained full independence from Britain two decades later, and one of its leaders, Jan Smuts, even played a leading role in creating the United Nations. Ethiopia was another exception. It was the only African kingdom to escape European colonization during the late 19th century; however, in 1950 it was still recovering from a brutal Italian occupation that had lasted from 1935 to 1941. Other African territories were under the rule of Great Britain, France, Portugal, Italy, and Spain, but by 1990 all of them would be fully independent.

It is risky to generalize about a region as large and diverse as Africa, but it should be evident that a central theme of the continent's modern history has been transitions from colonial subjugation to independence. Because of this, Africa's modern political leaders offer a particularly apt focus for exploring the changes through which the continent as a whole has gone. Although this book looks at only eight leaders from among the hundreds that Africa's 50-plus nations have produced, it covers a substantial sweep of modern African history. The leaders considered here represent all of the continent's major regions, and their stories provide representative examples of the changes and challenges that Africans have faced throughout the continent.

The chapters in this book are arranged according to the time frame in which each leader came to power. The book opens with a chapter on Haile Selassie, who became regent of Ethiopia in 1916 and emperor in 1930, and concludes with Nelson Mandela, who became president of South Africa in 1994. The chapters in between discuss Egypt's Gamal

Abdel Nasser (in power, 1952–70), Ghana's Kwame Nkrumah (1957–66), Senegal's Léopold Senghor (1960–81), Tanzania's Julius K. Nyerere (1961–85), Kenya's Jomo Kenyatta (1963–78), and Zimbabwe's Robert Mugabe (1980–   ).

A striking characteristic of modern African leaders has been how long they have held power. Six of the men discussed in this book died or left office after spending an average of nearly two dozen years in power—ranging from nine years for Nkrumah to 58 years for Haile Selassie. Compared to the long tenures of the others, Nkrumah's seems meager, yet he held power longer than any American president except Franklin D. Roosevelt. In general, Africans have tended to hold onto power until they die or are driven from office. Of the handful who have retired from office voluntarily, two are covered in this book: Senghor and Nyerere.

To appreciate the meaning of individual leaders' lives, it is necessary to understand the unique histories of the countries they ruled. To the casual observer one African country may look much like another. However, the differences among them are often marked. For example, Kenya and Tanzania are neighboring East African countries of similar size and natural assets, yet their political histories have been strikingly different. These differences are reflected in the lives of their first rulers, Kenyatta and Nyerere.

South Africa stands alone in African history in achieving its independence early in the 20th century and in being ruled from the start by a large, entrenched European population determined to reserve political power for itself. Moreover, South Africa's white government possessed such superior military power that its position seemed invulnerable to internal opposition. Mandela spent 27 years of his life as a political prisoner in a powerful state that never allowed an African to vote for a public official during his internment. However, because of relentless pressure, from both the country's African peoples and outside opponents, the government finally released him in 1990. Over the next few years the country underwent a political transformation that may be unparalleled in world history: In 1994 Mandela was elected president of the country.

Not all the stories in this book are as dramatic as that of Mandela, but each is unique for its own reasons. Each story also points up certain themes and patterns in one country that illuminate political changes in other countries as well. Egypt's Gamal Abdel Nasser, for example, is representative of political leaders in North Africa's largely Arabic-speaking Muslim countries. His story is also of interest because of Egypt's pivotal role in the tumultuous politics of the Middle East. Like some of the other leaders in this book, Nasser had a life that virtually encompassed the most significant political changes in his country's history. Born shortly after Britain declared a protectorate over Egypt, he grew up during a period of intense Egyptian nationalist fervor. Although Egypt formally regained its independence in 1922, it did not break completely free of British influence until Nasser himself cut the cord in 1956.

In all the other countries examined here, except Ethiopia and South Africa, the men profiled in this book led their countries to independence from European colonial rule. Most of them worked to win the right to vote for fellow Africans, but even in this regard their stories vary greatly. In Rhodesia (later, Zimbabwe), for example, Robert Mugabe was up against a settler regime that had vowed to retain white rule for a thousand years. In sharp contrast, the Senegal in which Léopold Senghor came of age was a colony of France in which some Africans had enjoyed the vote since the late 18th century. Moreover, France—quite unlike Britain—was tending to pull its colonies closer to itself. Successive French governments grappled with ideas of "assimilation," whereby peoples of colonies like Senegal would eventually adopt French culture and become French citizens themselves.

In the 20th century many Senegalese not only could vote, they sent elected deputies directly to France's National Assembly. Senghor himself was elected to the National Assembly after World War II. At the same time Africans in British colonies were struggling for representation on local government councils, Senghor was in Paris voting on policies that affected France itself; he even helped write France's national constitution. During the 1950s nationalist movements in Senegal and other colonies of French West Africa debated the desirability of closer association with France. When Charles de Gaulle let the colonies themselves vote on independence or remaining within the French Union, Senegal and most other colonies voted overwhelmingly to stay within the union.

The story of Haile Selassie also stands apart. As the heir to power in an independent monarchy, he represented a rare vestige of a traditional political system that survived into the 20th century. Much of his story concerns his efforts to modernize Ethiopia without sacrificing any of his personal power, and it is a story made all the more remarkable by the fact he held power for nearly six decades. His political career contrasts sharply with that of other African leaders of the late 20th century, but it is not without certain parallels. From 1936 to 1941 he went into exile while Fascist Italy occupied Ethiopia. After he was restored to power with the help of the British army he found his country in a quasi-colonial relationship with Britain that he was not about to abide.

On another level, these stories are also full of human interest. The ability of all of these leaders to overcome challenges says much about the human spirit. All of them achieved much of what they set out to do, but not all their stories have happy endings. However, questions about whether they succeeded or failed should probably be left for history to judge. Africa continues to change so rapidly that it will still take some time for the legacies of these rulers to be played out in full.

*Haile Selassie with U.S. president Lyndon B. Johnson during a state visit to the
United States in 1967* (Archive Photos)

Haile Selassie of Ethiopia

Early on a Thursday morning in September 1974—barely a month after Richard Nixon resigned the U.S. presidency—a tiny green Volkswagen sped through the deserted streets of Addis Ababa, Ethiopia's capital city. The few people who noticed the car saw something quite remarkable: Its cramped backseat contained the diminutive emperor who had ruled since long before most Ethiopians had been born. His mere presence in the humble Volkswagen was an extraordinary sight. It was also the *last* time he was seen in public.

Haile Selassie's quiet exit from power was a curious end to his long rule. Although the deposed 82-year-old emperor had reputedly been losing his grip, he did recognize how undignified his departure was. After he was taken from his palace and ordered to climb into the Volkswagen, he said, "You can't be serious. Am I supposed to go like *this*?"

It was the only protest he uttered that day.

In 1892—the year in which Haile Selassie was born—Ethiopia differed from the rest of Africa in many ways. Culturally, it straddled black Africa and the predominantly Muslim Middle East, but it was ruled by a Christian monarchy that claimed roots reaching back to the biblical Solomon and Sheba. Its Coptic national church was spiritually allied with the Orthodox Christian churches of Egypt and Greece.

Superficial physical characteristics distinguished Ethiopia's peoples from many of the black Africans living south of the Sahara Desert region, but these differences meant little to the outside world. Europeans in particular regarded Ethiopians as merely another group of black Africans who happened to have an ancient Christian culture.

The 1890s was a perilous time for the ancient Christian kingdom. Its rulers had been struggling for a century simply to hold the empire together in the face of nearly constant revolts mounted by Ethiopia's diverse peoples and numerous warlords. Emperor Menelik II had expanded the empire, but now it faced a new, external danger. At the time of Haile Selassie's birth, Italy was organizing colonies in Eritrea to Ethiopia's north and Somalia to Ethiopia's east, and the Italians coveted Ethiopia itself. For more than a decade Western European nations had been greedily grabbing African territories and building colonial empires. The process was an old one, but it had taken off in earnest in 1884, when European nations met in Berlin to draft ground rules for partitioning Africa among themselves. Representatives from African nations, however, were not invited to attend.

After the Berlin Conference, the partition of Africa proceeded so rapidly that by the turn of the century most of the continent was under European rule. France held most of West and Northwest Africa and part of Equatorial Africa; Great Britain held parts of West and East Africa, and much of Southern Africa; Portugal had Angola and Mozambique in Southern Africa and smaller colonies in West Africa; Belgium's King Leopold held the Congo (later Zaire); Germany had colonies in four different regions; and all of North Africa's Arab states—including Egypt—were under direct or indirect European rule.

Aside from the tiny West African republic of Liberia—founded in 1847 by former American slaves—Ethiopia was the only black African state to escape European colonialism. Preservation of its independence was not easy, however. In 1896 Italy made a major effort to conquer Ethiopia. At the Battle of Adowa Ethiopia inflicted on Italy the greatest military defeat that any European army ever suffered at the hands of Africans. The Ethiopian victory stopped the Italian advance, but it did not end the Italian quest to conquer Ethiopia.

Through the European scramble for Africa Emperor Menelik II not only preserved Ethiopia's independence, he enlarged its domains. He understood that for his country to survive, it had to modernize. A major reason his army defeated the Italians in 1896 was its use of modern firearms obtained from Italy in earlier negotiations.

Into this turbulent Ethiopian world Tafari Makonnen was born on July 23, 1892. He was christened Haile Selassie ("Power of the Trinity"), but was known as Tafari until he was crowned emperor in 1930. His birth took place in the predominantly Muslim province of Harar that his father, Ras Makonnen, governed. Makonnen's governorship was a particularly important one in the empire and the fact that he was a cousin and close adviser of Emperor Menelik ensured that the young Tafari would grow up amid the power politics of the empire and be groomed for political leadership.

In contrast to most sub-Saharan peoples, Ethiopia had long its own written language, but literacy was limited to the clergy and members of aristocratic families. Because of his

As I grew up the
spiritual desire was
guiding me to emulate
[my father] and so to
conduct myself that his
example should dwell
within me.

—Haile Selassie

family position Tafari was educated from an early age in both Amharic and the classic Ge'ez (or Ethiopic) languages, and he also learned the French language when he was tutored by a French missionary.

When Tafari was only 13 years old, his father gave him the title of *dejazmatch*—a rank of nobility similar to that of a European count. Tafari had good reason to expect that he would rise quickly within the imperial government's ranks. However, the unexpected death of his father in 1906 set back his chances. Nevertheless, Tafari had caught the attention of Emperor Menelik, who made him governor of part of the southern Sidamo Province when he was only 16 years old. Tafari performed so well in that position that Menelik gave him the governorship of the more important Harar Province just two years later.

A traditional mainstay in the Ethiopian political system was personal loyalty of officials to the emperors. Like his father, Tafari understood this well and served Menelik faithfully. When the emperor died in 1913, Tafari was disappointed not to be named heir, but did not hesitate to support Menelik's grandson, Iyasu V, who became emperor, although he himself was even younger than Tafari. Iyasu's reign was brief, however. He lacked the political maturity of Tafari and quickly alienated Christian leaders by indicating that he wanted to transform Ethiopia into a Muslim state. Tafari did not openly revolt against Iyasu, but he appears to have worked for his overthrow behind the scenes. In 1916 Iyasu was ousted and Menelik's 40-year-old daughter, Zawditu, became empress in September. Her accession to the throne had two conditions, however. She had to renounce her politically powerful husband, Ras Gugsa Wolie, and to accept Tafari as her regent and heir apparent.

Although Tafari did not become emperor himself until 1930, his rule of the country effectively dates from the beginning of his regency in September 1916, when he was 24 years old. Zawditu wore the crown, but Tafari held the real power, to which was added the title that his father had carried: *ras* (equivalent to a European duke). Over the next 14 years Ras Tafari Makonnen steadily established his personal control over Ethiopia, molding it into his own personal vision of a modern nation-state. His goal was to ensure the nation's survival by strengthening it from within and enhancing its position in the world at large. Through patience and persistence he would succeed in his goal, while retaining a near monopoly on political power for nearly six decades.

Tafari made a special effort to expand Ethiopia's almost nonexistent educational institutions in order to develop government officers better equipped to deal with the modern world. Ethiopia's educational advances were modest, even by the contemporary standards of colonial Africa, but they began producing the body of Western-educated people who were needed for the country to cope in the modern world. Tafari also worked to strengthen the central government, while reducing the power of outlying traditional chiefs and provincial administrators. One of his first tasks was to eliminate the threat of rebellion still posed by the ousted emperor Iyasu, who remained a fugitive until 1921.

The lessons that Ethiopia had learned in warding off Italian conquest in 1896 convinced Tafari of the need to build strong diplomatic relationships with the European nations. To do this, however, he had to convince them that Ethiopia deserved respect as a modern nation-state. Winning that respect was not an easy task, as most of the leaders of the Western nations looked down on Ethiopia as a backward country whose independence was due more to accident than the country's strengths. Moreover, if the Western nations acknowledged Ethiopia as a worthy member of the world community, they ran the risk of giving their African colonial subjects ideas about self-government. (Before World War II none of the colonial powers gave any serious thought to granting independence to African colonies.) In addition to these obstacles, Ethiopia had to face Western racism, which regarded black people as belonging to a distinctly lower order of humanity.

Creation of the League of Nations after World War I gave Tafari a concrete diplomatic goal—to win Ethiopia's admission to the league. This he achieved in 1923 by moving to eliminate the institution of slavery, which still pervaded Ethiopia, and by campaigning for Ethiopia's admission in diplomatic trips that he made to Europe.

Meanwhile, Tafari's steady accretion of power eventually alarmed Empress Zawditu. In 1928 he staged what amounted to a bloodless palace coup by forcing Zawditu to elevate him to *negus*—a title equivalent to king that would more clearly set him above everyone in the land but her. Two years later Zawditu's former husband, Ras Gugsa, raised an armed rebellion with the intent of forcing Tafari out. He evidently wanted to regain Zawditu's hand and have himself made emperor. Tafari dealt with this challenge efficiently; Tafari's troops defeated and killed Gugsa in October. Two days later Zawditu died.

Zawditu's sudden death caused some suspicion to fall on Tafari. However, she had already been gravely ill, and news of her former husband's death may well have been a fatal shock. In any case, Tafari had little reason to have Zawditu killed. He already held almost all political power within the empire. It had been just a question of time before he would inherit the title of emperor, and he had already proven that patience was one of his great strengths.

On November 2, 1930, Tafari, officially adopting his baptismal name of Haile Selassie, was crowned in Addis Ababa in an elaborate ceremony attended by representatives of many Western nations. During the following year he promulgated Ethiopia's first constitution, which established a parliament for the first time in the country's history.

Though he had achieved his ambition, Haile Selassie still faced great problems. During his long tenure as regent he had done much to quell rebellious tendencies within Ethiopia; however, the country's independence was still far from secure. Although Italy had failed to conquer the country in the 1890s, it had established colonies on Ethiopia's northern and eastern borders and still coveted Ethiopia itself. The 20th century brought many changes to modern warfare, increasing the gap in military power between Italy and Ethiopia. Haile Selassie did everything he could to obtain the weapons and training his country needed to build a modern army, but he got little help from the nations that could have provided it.

In the early 1920s Italy had fallen under the rule of Benito Mussolini's Fascist government, which soon hungered to build a colonial empire and to avenge the humiliation of the Battle of Adowa. When Italy began fabricating a border dispute with Ethiopia in late 1934, Haile Selassie desperately appealed to the League of Nations for help. The timing was unfortunate, however. While fascism was developing in Italy, Adolf Hitler's National Socialists were taking control of Germany and beginning to threaten neighboring countries. Some leaders in France and Great Britain recognized the justice of Ethiopia's claims against Italy, but they were more concerned with preserving peace in Europe than in seeing justice done in far-off Africa. In the mistaken belief that condoning Italy's invasion of Ethiopia would make Mussolini less likely to ally with Hitler, the Western European powers turned a blind eye toward Italy's conquest plans.

In October 1935 Italian forces rolled into Ethiopia from Eritrea. Ethiopia's national and provincial armies fiercely resisted the invasion, often winning pitched battles. Haile Selassie himself even went out in the field to command his troops personally. However, although the Italian advance was slow, its eventual success was never in doubt. The full weight of a modern European army was too much for the ancient African kingdom to resist. However, what ultimately enabled the Italians to prevail was the indiscriminate use of poison-gas bombs that their airplanes dropped on both military and civilian targets—in violation of the 1926 Geneva Convention that Italy had signed.

Although the Italians would never completely suppress all Ethiopian resistance, their main force steadily advanced toward Addis Ababa. In May 1936, with the invaders just

Haile Selassie (seated) and his family and retainers after leaving Addis Ababa in May 1936 (Archive Photos)

days from reaching the capital city, Haile Selassie accepted the advice of his councillors to go into exile, thereby defying a long tradition that required Ethiopian rulers to fall in battle. With a large retinue of relatives, he left Addis Ababa on May 2. A month later he reached London.

After establishing his exile headquarters in Great Britain, Haile Selassie went to Geneva, Switzerland, to address a session of the League of Nations. In a calmly dignified speech, he appealed for international help against Italy's bald aggression. Although his speech (delivered in Amharic, followed by a French translation) was hailed as an eloquent plea for the rights of small nations and the rule of international law, the league did nothing. Indeed, shortly afterward most of its members recognized Italy's sovereignty in Ethiopia, which the conquerors merged with Eritrea and Somaliland to form Italian East Africa.

Haile Selassie asked members of the League of Nations: If they did not come aid a weak fellow member now, who among would be next to fall? After World War II destroyed the League of Nations, many observers credited the league's failure to help Ethiopia as the beginning of its downfall.

Meanwhile, Haile Selassie and his family spent the next four years living quietly in Bath, England. There he might have remained indefinitely, had not World War II erupted in the fall of 1939. On June 10, 1940, as German troops advanced toward Paris, Italy joined the Axis powers (Germany and Japan) and declared war on the Allies, France and Great Britain. This hostile action suddenly transformed Italian East Africa into a military objective for the Allied forces. A month later Haile Selassie was in the Anglo-Egyptian Sudan. After the British organized and trained an Ethiopian-Sudanese invasion force to fight alongside its own units, Haile Selassie accompanied the combined forces into western Ethiopia early the following year.

Although Italy had a quarter of a million well-equipped troops in Ethiopia, Italian East Africa was ripe for invasion. Italy had never completely subdued the Ethiopians, and the Italian occupation troops had grown skittish. They were a long way from home, they had been worn down by guerrilla attacks, and they feared mass retaliation because of the brutality of their occupation. When the combined British-Ethiopian forces entered Ethiopia in January 1941, they met little serious resistance. On May 5—almost exactly five years after he had left Ethiopia—Haile Selassie triumphantly reentered Addis Ababa.

Back in his capital, Haile Selassie was not about to allow one European colonial power to replace another. He knew that the British, who regarded Italian East Africa as captured enemy territory, were not ready to restore Ethiopia's independence. However, Haile Selassie behaved as if he were fully in control. He moved quickly to evade British attempts to control his administration and began to court American aid to rebuild his military forces. The U.S. government was quick to support Ethiopia, and it later helped Ethiopia join the United Nations.

As World War II wound down in 1945, the U.S. State Department invited Haile Selassie to meet with President Franklin D. Roosevelt in Egypt, while the president was returning from the Yalta Conference. Haile Selassie used the meeting to outline his priorities for Ethiopia's future. These included unrestricted access to the sea, control over the railway line to Djibouti in French Somaliland, recovery of Eritrea, war reparations from Italy, and assistance to improve the military and create development projects.

The United States, in turn, welcomed Ethiopia as a valuable ally in a volatile part of the postwar world, especially when the Soviet Union began to compete with the United States as a rival superpower. The United States played a major role in the postwar decision of the United Nations to turn Eritrea over to Ethiopia. During the late spring of 1954 Haile Selassie visited the United States and addressed the U.S. Congress.

Ethiopia received U.S. military and development aid through the 1950s, but Haile Selassie was not satisfied with the levels of U.S. help. In 1959 he visited Europe's Soviet-dominated Eastern Bloc countries. He returned home with such generous offers of aid that the United States increased its support of Ethiopia to keep it from falling under Soviet influence at a time when many other black African nations were about to become independent.

American aid strengthened Haile Selassie's position within Ethiopia, allowing him to stave off growing demands for political reform. Despite his interest in modernizing his country, he resisted any real democratic changes. In 1955, for example, he granted a new constitution to celebrate his first quarter century as emperor. The new document created an elected house of parliament and gave the body some control over financial matters, but it took away little of the emperor's real power. If anything, Haile Selassie began tightening his grip on the government. A masterful manipulator of his ministers, he appointed to his cabinets members of rival factions; they would be more apt to ally with him than each other, ensuring that he alone remained in charge.

Dissatisfied with the pace of modernization, high-ranking members of the emperor's Imperial Guard launched a coup attempt while Haile Selassie was visiting South America in late 1960. On December 14 the coup leaders seized Addis Ababa's main radio station and had the emperor's son, Asfa Wossen, broadcast a speech calling for radical change. However, the coup was so poorly planned and executed that the emperor had little trouble putting it down on his return. Afterward, he attributed the rebellion to the misguided intentions of a minority of military officers and refused to recognize that their action reflected growing pressures for reform.

Resentment against Haile Selassie was particularly high in Eritrea, whose people had never accepted federation with Ethiopia with any enthusiasm. In 1960 Eritrean exiles living in Egypt announced the formation of the Eritrean Liberation Front. This organization would eventually win Eritrea's independence from Ethiopia in 1993. Meanwhile, another problem for Ethiopia arose in 1960 when Italian and British Somaliland merged to form the independent Republic of Somalia. The latent hostility between the Muslim Somali and Christian Amhara was aggravated by long-standing Somali claims on Ethiopia's eastern Ogaden Province. Somalia soon fell under the patronage of the Soviet Union, which helped it build a modern army with which to challenge Ethiopia.

Throughout the late 1960s and early 1970s conditions in Ethiopia gradually worsened. Drought and famine devastated rural areas; the national government spent increasing amounts of money combating insurgencies in Eritrea and other provinces; and external crises jolted Ethiopia's economy. By 1972, when Haile Selassie became 80 years old, his mental powers were clearly deteriorating. Around this time a disastrous famine was sweeping the north and he was evidently scarcely aware of its existence. In the face of this and other crises to which his government was not responding, it became clear to many Ethiopians that the time for revolutionary change had finally come. Throughout 1974 officers in the military carefully planned a coup.

> It became apparent to me during the course of conversation that Haile Selassie was already retreating into a dream world. . . . the curtain of senility had dropped.
>
> —American adviser John H. Spencer

Early on the morning of September 12 a few military officers drove to the royal palace and read to the emperor a proclamation of his deposition as emperor. Maintaining his dignified bearing, as always, Haile Selassie said that he would accept the proclamation, so long as it was for the good of the people. He was then led to a green Volkswagen, which carried him off. From that moment he was never again seen in public. On August 28, 1975—almost a year later—the national radio station announced that he had died.

Chronology

July 23, 1892	Tafari Makonnen (Haile Selassie) is born in Ethiopia's Harar Province
1906	his father, Ras Makonnen, dies
1908	Tafari is appointed governor of part of Sidamo Province
1910	is appointed governor of Harar Province
1913	Emperor Menelik dies and is succeeded by his grandson, Iyasu V
1916	Tafari is named a *ras* and regent after a coup replaces Iyasu with Empress Zawditu
1923	leads Ethiopia into the League of Nations
1924	tours Egypt, the Holy Land, and Western Europe
1928	forces Zawditu to name him *negus*
1930	is crowned emperor with the regal name Haile Selassie
1931	promulgates Ethiopia's first constitution
1935	Italy invades Ethiopia
1936–40	Haile Selassie goes into exile in England

1936	addresses League of Nations
1941	takes part in British invasion of Ethiopia
1945	consults with U.S. president Franklin D. Roosevelt in Egypt
1952	Eritrea is federated with Ethiopia
1954	Haile Selassie visits the United States
1955	creates Ethiopia's first national assembly
1959	visits Eastern Bloc countries
1960	Imperial Guard attempts a coup while Haile Selassie tours South America
1963	Haile Selassie oversees establishment of Organization of African Unity in Addis Ababa
1973	attempts to cover up famine in northern provinces; inflation causes major anti-government demonstrations
1974	is deposed by the military
August 27, 1975	Haile Selassie dies in Addis Ababa

Further Reading

Haile Selassie I. *My Life and Ethiopia's Progress: The Autobiography of Emperor Haile Selassie I, 1892–1937*. Edited and translated by Edward Ullendorff. New York: Oxford University Press, 1976. First of Haile Selassie's two autobiographical volumes to be translated into English.

Marcus, Harold G. *Haile Sellassie I: The Formative Years, 1892–1936*. Berkeley: University of California Press, 1987. First of a projected three-part biography by the leading American authority on Ethiopian history. A clear and inviting book to read.

———. *A History of Ethiopia*. Berkeley: University of California Press, 1994. Lucid survey of modern Ethiopian history, with close attention to Haile Selassie's role.

Negash, Askale. *Haile Selassie*. New York: Chelsea House, 1989. Well-illustrated critical biography for young adult readers by an Ethiopian educated in the United States.
Prouty, Chris, and Eugene Rosenfeld. *Historical Dictionary of Ethiopia and Eritrea*. 2d ed. Metuchen, N.J.: Scarecrow Press, 1994. Encyclopedic reference with handy entries on persons, places, events, and other subjects relating to Haile Selassie.

*Anxious to be seen as a pan-African, as well as a pan-Arab, leader, Nasser in-
volved himself in African affairs. Here he entertains Ethiopian emperor Haile
Selassie (left) and President Julius K. Nyerere of Tanzania (right).* (Archive
Photos/LDE)

Gamal Abdel Nasser of Egypt

In June 1967 Egyptian president Gamal Abdel Nasser expected to savor a military victory over Israel. Since coming to power 15 years earlier, he had vowed to avenge the humiliation that Israel had inflicted on Egypt in 1948. So confident of success was he now that he drew other Arab nations to his side and provoked Israel to start a fight. Israel attacked, as Nasser expected, but with unexpected suddenness and fury. Within hours Israeli planes annihilated the air forces of Egypt, Syria, and Iraq. In six days Israel shattered Egypt's army and occupied the Sinai Peninsula.

Egypt's defeat was total. Although poor planning, poor military leadership, and overconfidence provided blame enough for many, Nasser saw no point in blaming others. On national television he proclaimed himself solely responsible for the disaster and resigned. To his surprise, hundreds of thousands of Egyptians took to the streets to demand he not resign. By the end of the day, he was back in office—more popular than ever.

If there is today a nation that can at once be called young *and* very, very old, it is Egypt. Its roots as a nation stretch back nearly five thousand years—even before its great pyramids were built. Its independence as a modern nation, however, can be measured only in decades. Despite the grandeur that was ancient Egypt, the country fell under foreign rule in the fourth century B.C. and did not fully regain its independence until the mid-20th century. Through the centuries Greeks, Romans, Arabs, Turks, the French, and, finally, the British ruled Egypt.

After all these conquests, the one foreign culture that stuck was Arab. Egypt was one of the first countries to fall to conquerors coming out of the Arabian Peninsula during the seventh century. Along with most of the rest of North Africa, it afterward retained the Arabic language and the new Islamic religion, and its peoples came to think of themselves as Arabs.

Early invaders coveted Egypt's agricultural produce, made bountiful by the annual floods of the mighty Nile River. Later invaders sought to control Egypt because of its strategic position. Located at the southeastern corner of the Mediterranean Sea, Egypt has long been a busy crossroads for traders, travelers, religious pilgrims, and military conquerors. Its location became even more important in 1869, after the Suez Canal was built across the isthmus connecting Egypt's African and Asian regions. By linking the Mediterranean and Red Seas, the canal spared ships sailing between Europe and Asia the long voyage around Africa. Indeed, Great Britain regarded the canal as such a vital link in its own empire that it occupied Egypt in 1882. Though the British claimed they did not want to stay, they declared a protectorate over Egypt in 1914, then ruled the country much as they did their other colonies.

In 1919—a year after Gamal Abdel Nasser was born— Egypt entered a long period of political turmoil. When Great

Britain refused to grant Egypt independence, a revolutionary movement sprang up. Over the next four decades one patriotic goal overrode all others: ending all British influence. From a relatively early age, helping to attain that goal would become one of Nasser's central ambitions.

In 1922 Britain ended its protectorate, making Egypt independent under a constitutional monarch, King Fuad I. Britain did not, however, relinquish all control. It left a large military force behind and reserved the right to oversee foreign interests in Egypt, particularly in the Suez Canal zone. This settlement satisfied few Egyptians. A nationalist party, the Wafdi, continued to demand full independence, and the new king wanted to rule without constitutional oversight.

Two years later Britain's top military commander in Egypt was assassinated and Britain again tightened its grip on the country. However, continuous Egyptian protests eventually moved Britain to grant more substantial concessions to nationalists. A new treaty in 1936 called for Britain to remove its troops from everywhere in Egypt except the canal zone, where they could stay for 20 years. Egypt still remained far from fully independent.

The man who would eventually lead Egypt to full independence, Gamal Abdel Nasser, was born in the port city of Alexandria on January 15, 1918. He was the first of four sons of Abdel Nasser Hussein, a government postal clerk. Little is known about his mother, except that she died young. Because the government frequently reassigned his father to new towns, he had no stable home until he was seven and his father sent him to live with an uncle in Cairo. There he began his formal education.

Not a good student in his early youth, Nasser was remembered as naturally rebellious. For example, when his father ordered him not to dig in the garden, he dug such a deep hole that his father fell in. Eventually, however, he became more serious about his studies and developed a special interest in reading biographies of great historical figures. Growing up at a time when Egyptian patriotism and anti-British feeling pervaded Egypt, he developed an early interest in politics. By the mid-1930s he was leading anti-British demonstrations in Cairo. These demonstrations peaked in November 1935, when Nasser saw two friends killed in street fighting and was himself wounded in the head by a bullet.

After finishing secondary school Nasser began studying law, but soon gave this up and joined the army. At first his role in the late 1935 demonstrations kept him out of the Royal Military Academy, but in 1937 he was among the 40 students admitted (out of more than 400 applicants). At the academy Nasser finally came into his own. He did well academically and became known as an outspoken opponent of colonialism. After graduating in July 1938 he was posted at Mankabâd in central Egypt as a platoon commander.

Nasser's early military service coincided with the early years of World War II (1939–45). North Africa became a major theater of the war and Britain and Germany fought a decisive battle at El Alamein in northern Egypt in 1942. Nevertheless, the war had little direct impact on Nasser. Through those years, as he was transferred among several posts and returned to the military academy as a teacher, he grew increasingly unhappy with conditions in the Egyptian army, government inefficiency, and the continued presence of British troops.

In February 1942 an incident occurred that strengthened the resolve of Nasser and other Egyptian patriots to get rid of the British. When King Farouk (who had succeeded his father, King Fuad I, in 1936) dismissed the government that Britain favored, the local high commissioner ordered British troops to surround the royal palace until the king accepted a Wafdist cabinet under Nahas Pasha. Nasser vowed to avenge this humiliation.

During the war years Nasser began secretly organizing a group he called the Free Officers—army men dedicated to winning complete independence for Egypt and achieving social justice. It would be a decade before this group took action, but their eventual success demonstrated Nasser's extraordinary patience and organizing abilities. He alone knew the identity of all the Free Officers.

Anti-British feeling remained high in Egypt after the war and grew even stronger in 1948, when Britain relinquished its protectorate over neighboring Palestine, allowing Jewish settlers to create the state of Israel. Egypt joined the other Arab states in declaring war on Israel, but its performance in the ensuing war was dismal. Nasser—by then a major—was one of the few Egyptian officers to distinguish himself in that conflict. Though badly wounded, he saved his battalion from obliteration at Faluja (near Jerusalem) when a large part of the Egyptian army was besieged for several months by the Israelis.

Nasser blamed Egypt's miserable performance in the war on the failure of King Farouk's government to provide adequate equipment and he renewed his vow to bring about change. At Faluja he called the first meeting of the Free Officers and set in motion plans for revolution. These men, who eventually numbered about 700, began quietly infiltrating the leadership positions in the military, the government, and even the royal palace.

In 1950 Egypt was in greater political disarray than ever. The Wafdi party won the national elections, but King Farouk was pressing to exercise greater power himself and antigovernment demonstrations and assassinations were rocking the country, largely because of the continued presence of the British military at the Suez Canal. Anti-British feeling reached a peak in late 1951, by which time Egyptian-British clashes were turning into a small war. At the same time, King Farouk attempted to manipulate elections in the army's private officers club, further alienating members of the Free Officers. In July 1952 Farouk finally went too far when he tried to appoint his own brother-in-law minister of war.

On July 23 Nasser's Committee of Free Officers seized control of the government in a carefully planned coup in which no blood was shed. Forced to abdicate, King Farouk went into permanent exile, and his infant son, Fuad II, was named king. Understanding that the populace would be reluctant to accept the leadership of young army officers, Nasser arranged to have the popular General Muhammad Naguib made head of the new government's Council of the Revolution. A year later Egypt was proclaimed a republic with Naguib as president and Nasser as vice president, and the infant king was dismissed.

During the first few years of the revolution Nasser was content to let Naguib be the nominal head of the government and later head of state. The two leaders' titles changed several times, but Nasser himself was always in charge. Eventually he and Naguib had an irreconcilable falling out over the question of transforming Egypt into a parliamentary democracy, a step that Naguib favored. In late 1954 Nasser finally ended the struggle by having Naguib arrested and making himself the head of the government. (Naguib remained imprisoned until after Nasser's death, in 1971.)

I have been a conspirator for so long that I mistrust all around me.

—Gamal Abdel Nasser

Nasser's opposition to introducing parliamentary democracy to Egypt stemmed from his insistence on first achieving what he regarded as the revolution's primary goals: Egypt's complete independence and the creation of social justice. During his long years of preparing for the revolution Nasser devoted most of his energy to planning and organizing, paying relatively little attention to developing a coherent revolutionary philosophy. He wanted to restore Egyptian independence and dignity and to create greater political and social equality, but he otherwise lacked clear goals. Having come to power without a definite philosophy, he was inclined to respond harshly to political opponents. He made Egypt a one-party state but the philosophy of "Arab Socialism" that he eventually proclaimed was never a precise political doctrine.

Nasser's first significant achievement was negotiation of a new settlement with Britain over the Suez Canal. In October 1954 he got Britain to agree to withdraw completely from the canal within 20 months. This agreement merely confirmed promises that Britain had made in 1936, but it enhanced Nasser's prestige and increased his ability to institute political and economic reforms within Egypt. As he was negotiating with Britain, his government was working to give Egyptian peasants farmland seized from the rich.

The prestige that Nasser won from his settlement with Britain helped make him a leading figure at the conference of nonaligned nations that he attended in Bandung, Indonesia, in 1955. (The nonaligned nations basically avoided taking sides in the cold war between the United States and the Soviet Union, while accepting aid from both the rival superpowers.) From that point he took a greater interest in world affairs and worked to give Egypt a leading place in international councils. He eventually sought to make Egypt the center of three circles: the Arab world, the Muslim world, and Africa.

The year 1956 proved to be a turning point as important as 1952 had been. While searching for help to develop Egypt, Nasser had signed a 1955 trade agreement with the Soviet Union and made a large arms purchase from Czechoslovakia —moves that made the Western nations suspicious of his nonalignment claims. All the same, in mid-1956 Britain fulfilled its agreement with Egypt by removing its last troops from the canal zone, just before Nasser was elected president under a new constitution. At this time Egypt was negotiating with Britain and the United States for loans with which to build a huge dam on the upper Nile. The Aswan High Dam was to fulfill the ancient Egyptian dream of regulating the Nile's annual floodwaters. In the absence of major oil deposits or mineral wealth, the country depended on its agricultural production, which in turn depended on the unpredictable flow of the Nile.

In July Britain and the United States, apparently miffed with Egypt because of its Soviet bloc connections, told Nasser they would not help finance the Aswan Dam. Nasser then took what was perhaps the boldest step in his career by announcing that Egypt would nationalize the Suez Canal and use its revenues to finance the dam. At issue was not ownership of the canal—Egypt already owned it—but its control. Until then the canal had been operated by the French-owned Suez Canal Company, whose concession was not due to expire until 1968. Although international law recognized the right of nations to nationalize property within their own borders, Britain and France denounced Egypt's action and threatened invasion. In October, Israel—which also depended on the canal—joined Britain and France in attacking Egypt.

In a war that lasted just over a week, Israel occupied the Sinai Peninsula and British and French bombers wiped out the Egyptian air force. To the allies' surprise, however, world opinion rallied behind Egypt, and the United States and the Soviet Union joined in pressing them to halt their aggression. From what had threatened to be a disaster, Egypt emerged victorious and Nasser's prestige reached even greater heights. With this achievement, it might be said that he finally won Egypt its full independence.

With the issue of the Suez Canal settled, Nasser turned his attention to his goal of Arab unity. At his urging the leaders

Nasser (second from left) and Soviet premier Nikita Khrushchev (third from left) at May Day celebration in Moscow in 1958 (Archive Photos)

of Syria agreed to merge their country with Egypt. In February 1958 the two countries came together as the United Arab Republic (UAR), with Nasser as president. Tiny Yemen joined in March. The union was never close; it dissolved three years later, although Egypt officially continued to call itself the United Arab Republic until after Nasser's death. Nasser tried later to unite with other Arab nations, but none of these efforts came to anything. During the 1960s, however, he played leading roles in the Arab League, the Organization of African Unity, and other international bodies.

In 1962 Nasser increased the government's involvement in the economy by nationalizing banks, insurance companies, and other firms, and having companies turn over half their capital to the government. Although his efforts to socialize the economy produced no clear economic gains, he was popularly perceived to be a champion of the poor. Through this period he turned increasingly to the Soviet bloc for economic aid, and got the Soviet Union to underwrite the enormous cost of building the Aswan Dam, which was completed in 1968.

Meanwhile, Nasser still rankled over Egypt's past humiliations at the hands of Israel. In his role as the leading spokesperson for the Arab nations he also wished to take a stand on the Palestinian Arab homeland question. In early 1967 he began challenging Israel. He demanded that the United Nations remove its troops from the positions they had occupied since 1956 and announced that Egypt was closing the Gulf of Aqaba to Israeli shipping, thus severing Israel's only direct link to the Red Sea. Outwardly confident of victory in any war with Israel, Nasser worked up Egyptian sentiment against the Jewish state and persuaded the leaders of Syria and Iraq to join Egypt in crushing Israel.

Despite Nasser's confidence, Egypt was not well prepared for war. Moreover, he failed to take into account how seriously the Israelis took his threats. Surrounded by belligerent Arab nations and fearing for its own survival, Israel made meticulous preparations for war and struck first. In what became known as the Six-Day War, Israel overwhelmed the military forces of all its Arab opponents and occupied Egypt's Sinai Peninsula, Jordan's West Bank, and Syria's Golan Heights.

> Whatever the faults of others may be, my responsibility in the defeat is total. . . . I no longer claim to be the leader of my people.
>
> —Gamal Abdel Nasser

Although Egypt suffered a crushing defeat in the war, Nasser emerged with his popularity largely undamaged. However, during the three years that remained in his life, he had to meet growing public demands for democratizing the government.

For all his apparent belligerence in the two wars Egypt fought with Israel under his leadership, Nasser was not at heart a warmonger. His experience in the 1948 war soured him on violence and probably contributed to the generally peaceful methods he used to win and maintain political power. During the last year of his life he accepted an American proposal to negotiate a political settlement with Israel. He did not live to achieve that, but his successor, Anwar Sadat—one of his old Free Officer colleagues—did make that breakthrough later.

On September 28, 1970, Nasser died in his home outside Cairo. Beset by diabetes, circulatory problems, and the strains of office, he succumbed to a heart attack at the age of 52. The legacy of his 18 years in power was mixed, but the spontaneous outpouring of grief by millions of Egyptians was real. Whatever his limitations, he is still revered for restoring Egyptian independence and pride.

Chronology

January 15, 1918	Gamal Abdel Nasser is born in Alexandria
1936	is suspended from school for participating in a political demonstration
1937–38	attends Royal Military Academy
1938	begins army career as a second lieutenant
1943	teaches at the Royal Military Academy
1945	establishes contacts with future Free Officers
1948–49	fights in war with Israel
1952	leads coup that ousts King Farouk

1954	publishes *The Philosophy of Revolution*; takes full power as premier and military governor of Egypt
1955	attends Bandung Conference in Indonesia
1956	is elected president of Egypt; nationalizes the Suez Canal Company, provoking Israeli and Anglo-French invasion
1958	becomes president of the United Arab Republic, formed from merger of Egypt and Syria
1961	Syria withdraws from UAR
1962	Nasser redefines his "socialism" in the form of a charter and projects a democratic regime
1965	is reelected president with 99.9 percent majority
1967	Egypt fights Six-Day War against Israel
1968	Aswan High Dam is completed
September 28, 1970	Gamal Abdel Nasser dies of a heart attack in Cairo

Further Reading

DeChancie, John. *Gamal Abdel Nasser*. New York: Chelsea House, 1988. Biography in Chelsea's series on world leaders for young adult readers.

Goldschmidt, Arthur, Jr. *Historical Dictionary of Egypt*. Metuchen, N.J.: Scarecrow Press, 1994. Useful handbook for people, places, and events in Nasser's life.

Lacouture, Jean. *Nasser: A Biography*. New York: Alfred A. Knopf, 1973. Intimate biography by a French journalist who knew Nasser personally.

Sanderson, Frank. *Nasser*. Harlow, England: Longman, 1974. Short biography written for British schoolchildren.

Shimoni, Yaacov. *Biographical Dictionary of the Middle East*. New York: Facts On File, 1991. Useful guide to Nasser and other Egyptian figures, written by Israeli scholars.

Copies of this official portrait of Kwame Nkrumah hung in every government office and in many homes while he was in power. (Archive Photos)

Kwame Nkrumah of Ghana

During the late 1940s, a young West African returned home to the Gold Coast Colony apprehensively. During 12 years abroad he had gained a reputation as a leftist agitator. Knowing well how hard Great Britain worked to keep radical ideas out of its colonies, he had good reason to expect trouble from immigration officials. At Takoradi the official to whom he handed over his passport happened to be an African, but that was small comfort. The man did not even open the passport; he simply stared at its cover, amazed by the name he saw. Finally, he whispered: "So *you* are Kwame Nkrumah!"

Nkrumah nodded uncomfortably, expecting the worst—especially when the official led him away. Once they were alone, however, the man seized Nkrumah's hand, pumped it, and raved about how much he had heard about him and how grateful their countrymen were that he was returning to help his people.

A small irony in African history is the fact that West Africa, the region in which European imperialism began the earliest, was also the part of Africa in which Europe made the least efforts to establish white settlements. The reasons lay in climate and population distribution. In comparison with much of eastern and southern Africa, West Africa was hotter, more humid, and more densely populated by Africans—and thus less inviting to European settlement. Even more important, Europeans succumbed so readily to tropical diseases in West Africa that the region became known as the "white man's grave." Indeed, Nkrumah would one day propose—and only partly in jest—that a monument be erected to the anopheles mosquito, the carrier of the deadly malaria bacterium that contributed so greatly to keeping Europeans out of West Africa.

When West Africans began clamoring for their independence in the mid-20th century, the colonial powers could negotiate with them without having to take into account the same kinds of vested European settler interests that complicated independence movements in other parts of Africa. In a sense, this was imperialism in its purest form: alien rule over subject peoples who lacked ties to the ruling country.

From the late 15th century through the 19th century, European ships sailed the West African coast, trading for ivory, gold, and human beings. They did most of their business near the coastline, leaving local African states to connect with suppliers farther inland. Occasionally, Europeans established permanent bases at coastal ports, and some of these became the starting points for the colonies that were created toward the end of the 19th century. The borders of West Africa's modern nations reflect the way in which the colonies were carved out. In most cases, the European powers started at the coast and simply pushed directly inland, with little regard for existing ethnic divisions. Many borders thus simply run inland, like spokes on a bicycle wheel. Such, indeed, was the case of the Gold Coast, which took its name from the lucrative gold trade for which it was long known.

When Kwame Nkrumah returned to the Gold Coast in 1947, most of tropical Africa was under European rule and no plans were afoot to set any colony on the road to independence. Within a decade, however, Nkrumah would become prime minister of an independent Ghana. As the first African to lead a nation to independence he made himself a model for other nationalist leaders, a fact lending a special importance to his life story.

Ghana has a comparatively homogenous culture. Most Ghanaians speak Twi languages, whose major branches include the Akan cluster—which encompasses Ghana's large Ashanti, Fante, and Baule subgroups—as well as a cluster spilling over into the Ivory Coast. That latter cluster includes the tiny Nzima group into which Nkrumah was born. Nkrumah was thus culturally affiliated with the majority of Ghana's people, but was not a member of a major group. This fact later contributed to his favoring a strong unitary national state.

Nkroful, the Gold Coast village into which Nkrumah was born, lies near the Atlantic coast, roughly midway between Takoradi and the Ivory Coast border. The dates most often assigned to his birth are September 18 and 21, 1909; one of these may be correct, but each is only an informed guess.

Little is known of Nkrumah's father, except that he was a fine goldsmith and had several wives, as did many prosperous Africans. He died while Nkrumah was young. Nkrumah's mother, Elizabeth Nyanibah, was a successful trader, and he stayed close to her into his adult life. Although Nkrumah's parents were illiterate, they recognized he was bright and sent him to nearby Roman Catholic schools at an early age. He did so well at the school at Half Assini that he was kept on as a pupil-instructor when he was about 17. Around that same time the principal of the colony's prestigious Achimota College visited the school and recruited Nkrumah as a student.

Achimota was one of the most progressive schools in West Africa. Its students were not afraid to discuss such heady matters as self-government, so Nkrumah naturally began growing interested in political issues. After earning his teaching certificate from Achimota in 1930, he spent several years teaching at different schools. He was recognized as a brilliant teacher, but also showed signs of political leadership by helping to organize a teachers' union. He might have remained a teacher indefinitely, had he not decided to follow the footsteps of the Nigerian journalist and nationalist leader Benjamin Azikiwe by going to the United States to attend Pennsylvania's Lincoln University. The journey was expensive, so Nkrumah called on a relative in Nigeria for financial help after stowing away on a freighter. In the fall of 1935 he left Nigeria for America. He happened to pass through London at the moment that word of Italy's invasion of Ethiopia arrived. Until then Ethiopia had stood as the supreme surviving symbol of African independence so the news was devastating.

In starting a career as a teacher before getting into politics, Nkrumah resembled many members of Africa's first generation of modern political leaders. What set him apart from others was his experience of living in the United States for 10 years, and particularly his experience of living among African Americans. Lincoln University, founded shortly after the Civil War, was then an all-black institution. There Nkrumah started reading the works of Marcus Garvey (the self-styled "provisional president of Africa"), W. E. B. Du Bois, and other black writers. He also visited and lived among the large African-American communities in cities such as Philadelphia and New York, and spent his summers working on freighters. These experiences broadened his view of the world and contributed to the later development of his pan-African ideology.

In 1939 Nkrumah graduated in sociology and economics from Lincoln. He then entered Lincoln's theology seminary while simultaneously studying philosophy and education at the University of Pennsylvania, which was 50 miles distant. He earned a bachelor's degree in theology at Lincoln in 1942 and a master's degree at Penn the following year. He then started a doctoral program at Penn, but was so worn down by traveling between the two universities and working in a shipyard that he dropped out. Meanwhile, however, he undertook his first overly political project by helping to found the African Students' Association of America and Canada, of which he was elected president. He used some of his new free time to organize his ideas on African economic and political conditions in a pamphlet, *Towards Colonial Freedom*, which he later published in London.

In May 1945, as the winding down of World War II made transatlantic travel safe again, Nkrumah sailed from New York to England. This English phase of his life was a brief one, but it played a crucial role in his political career. He arrived in London intending to study law but got caught up in the vibrant political atmosphere prevailing among students, writers, and political organizers from other African and West Indian colonies. He joined the West African Students' Union and soon abandoned his studies in favor of political work. While helping to organize the Fifth Pan-African Conference in Manchester in October, he worked along-

Africa is the beloved of his [Nkrumah's] dreams; philosopher, thinker, with forceful schemes.

—Nkrumah's Lincoln University yearbook

side such figures as Du Bois (who later became a citizen of Ghana) and Kenya's future president Jomo Kenyatta. Afterward he became the secretary of a new London-based West African nationalist organization. In this capacity he began publishing a newspaper, *The New African*, which promoted African unity, particularly among the West African colonies. The paper proved influential enough to be banned by the government of the Gold Coast.

While Nkrumah had been abroad the Gold Coast prospered. The colony's mining industries and cocoa plantations were flourishing, and Africans were beginning to have some direct representation in the colony's legislative council. With Britain and France beginning to liberate their Asian colonies, independence no longer seemed an impossible goal for African peoples. The Gold Coast itself was a prime candidate for self-government: Its economy was developing rapidly, and it had comparatively good schools and growing numbers of well-educated people ready to assume leadership positions. Moreover, there was no local settler community poised to challenge Africans for political supremacy. In this environment, a group of educated Africans got together under the leadership of Joseph B. Danquah in 1947 and founded the United Gold Coast Convention (UGCC), a political party dedicated to attaining self-government through constitutional means.

UGCC leaders had little practical experience in political organizing and Nkrumah was building a reputation as an effective organizer, so they invited him to return home and become their party's general secretary. Nkrumah accepted the invitation and left London in November 1947. When he reached Takoradi the following month, he was pleasantly surprised to find many of his countrypeople (including the immigration officer) waiting to welcome him home warmly. The UGCC then had only a trifling membership in a handful of branches, so he immediately set about traversing the country to build up the party.

The year 1948 was a difficult one for the colony. It began with an attempt at a nationwide boycott of Syrian and European merchants whose prices Africans believed were too high. The government was also angering cocoa farmers by pressuring them to diversify their crops. Although the boycott was called off, rioting developed in Accra and 29 people were killed. Seeking a scapegoat for the disturbances, the government arrested Nkrumah for violating a law against political agitation. The experience transformed him into a political martyr and enhanced his popularity, teaching him the value of adding "P.G."—prison graduate—after his name.

By mid-1949 the conservative leaders of the UGCC regarded Nkrumah as too radical for their party, so they pushed him out. He responded by forming a new body, the Convention People's Party (CPP), which was unabashedly dedicated to winning immediate self-government. In the fall he launched the "positive action" campaign, using labor strikes and nonviolent protests to prod the government into making political concessions. As political tensions mounted in the colony, the government declared a state of emergency and again arrested Nkrumah.

While Nkrumah was imprisoned, a new constitution went into effect, granting greatly increased political authority to Africans. In early 1951 the CPP won 35 of the 38 legislative seats contested in a general election. The colonial administration had no choice but to release Nkrumah and make him "leader of government business" (this title was upgraded to "prime minister" the following year). From that moment, the Gold Coast's future independence was not in doubt. Nkrumah's exuberant followers carried him through Accra's streets in triumph, and he delivered a speech making lavish promises of full employment, free education,

Seek ye first the political kingdom, and all things else shall be added unto you.

—Kwame Nkrumah

industrialization, national health service, and even free public transportation.

The CPP swept national elections again in 1954, but this time the party faced a challenge from the National Liberation Front (NLF), an outgrowth of the old UGCC. Based in the important Ashanti region of the country, the NLF opposed Nkrumah's call for a strong unitary state, instead favoring a federal system that would protect regional interests. To test national political preferences the colonial administration called for new general elections in mid-1956. Nkrumah opposed this step, but his party again won, putting him in an even stronger position. Britain now had no choice but to promise independence.

On March 6, 1957, the Gold Coast became independent as the nation of Ghana. Ghana took its new name from an empire that had flourished centuries earlier in the inland Sudanic region. The old Ghana Empire had nothing to do with the new Ghanaian nation, but its name recalled a past age of African glory and was intended to point to an even more glorious future. For Nkrumah, that future lay in African unity.

Nkrumah quickly set about harnessing Ghana's resources to promote continental unity. Over the next several years he convened two pan-African conferences and toured Africa to promote his ideas. He scored a small success in 1958, when France suddenly granted independence to nearby Guinea. The French offered Guinea very little material help, and Nkrumah came forward with a loan of $25 million. He and Guinean president Sékou Touré joined their countries together—though only on paper. Meanwhile, Nkrumah was busy setting in motion major improvements in Ghana's

Kwame Nkrumah arrives in London for a Commonwealth conference in early 1960—a year in which most of Ghana's West African neighbors became independent. (Archive Photos/Central Press)

national education system and social services. He also began committing the government to investments in huge prestige projects, the most successful of which would be a hydroelectric dam on the Volta River.

Africa remembers 1960 as the year of independence. That year, in which 17 countries became free, was also a turning point in Ghana's freedom. Nkrumah had been losing his patience with political opponents and had been increasing his powers as prime minister. In a July 1960 referendum (which some observers charged was rigged) Ghanaians voted to make Ghana a republic, with Nkrumah as president. With many of the restraints imposed by the original constitution gone, Nkrumah declared himself the "Keeper of the Nation's Conscience and Fount of Honour" and assumed new powers over the legislature, national judiciary, and the ruling CPP. He also began taking over newspapers and broadcasting stations in order to control the dissemination of news.

With his increased powers Nkrumah was able to turn his attention more fully to promoting his dream of uniting Africa. He found, however, that leaders of the new nations were not interested in surrendering any of their newly won sovereignty. Moreover, the many challenges they faced in their own countries made ideas about continental unity seem lofty and ridiculous. Nkrumah's prestige began eroding, and it became clear that he was neglecting problems in his own country.

Part of Nkrumah's vision for Africa was his faith in promoting industrialization over the agriculture on which Ghana's past prosperity had been largely based. In 1959 he issued an economic development plan that called for heavy state involvement and favored expensive industrial schemes. Within two years, however, it was clear that the plan was failing. When a nationwide labor strike erupted in protest against government policies, Nkrumah used massive police and military force to crush it.

In August 1962 someone tossed a grenade at Nkrumah in northern Ghana. Nkrumah was uninjured, but four others were killed and another 50 injured. The incident devastated him; some have said that it broke his heart. As more incidents of violence were directed against Nkrumah and his supporters, he became reclusive and took increasingly harsh measures to protect himself. He created a private regiment to serve as his bodyguard and had many people—including some of his own ministers—arrested and imprisoned without trial.

The year 1964 began with an attempt on Nkrumah's life by a member of the police detail guarding his residence. Nkrumah purged the police. He also accused his former

UGCC boss, Joseph Danquah, of complicity and had him sent to prison, where he died the following year. Meanwhile, Nkrumah declared himself president for life and outlawed all opposition parties. By this time he liked to be known as Osagyefo, the "Redeemer."

By 1966 Nkrumah's economic policies had placed the country deeply in debt. Hundreds of political opponents were in prison, and Ghana's government was widely regarded as greedy and corrupt. In February Nkrumah paid a state visit to Beijing, China, with the purpose of mediating a settlement in the growing Vietnam War. On February 24 army officers arrested his ministers in Ghana and announced that Nkrumah was deposed. They justified the coup by charging that Nkrumah had stolen massive amounts of money from the country.

Pent-up anger against Nkrumah quickly rose to the surface in Ghana. Thousands of people paraded in the streets to celebrate his fall, carrying anti-Nkrumah signs and pulling down the many statues he had erected to himself. The journalists he had jailed were released from prison and restored to their former positions, which they used to add their voices to the chorus of angry condemnation.

Without trying to return to Ghana from China, Nkrumah took up residence in Guinea, where his old friend Sékou Touré made him honorary copresident. He spent his last years writing books that attempted to apply Marxist political theory to Africa. On April 27, 1972, he died of cancer in a hospital in Bucharest, Romania, where he had gone for treatment. He was 63 years old.

Nkrumah could have been a great man. He started well . . . Somewhere down the line, however . . . he developed a strange love for absolute power.

—Akwasi A. Afrifa

Although he was still unpopular in Ghana, his body was returned home for burial.

Chronology

September 18 or 21, 1909	Francis Nwia (Kwame) Nkrumah is born in Nkroful, Gold Coast
1927–30	studies at Achimota College
1930–34	teaches at several schools
1935–45	studies in the United States
1945–47	lives in London
1947	publishes *Towards Colonial Freedom*; returns to Gold Coast
1948	begins working as general secretary of the UGCC; is arrested and jailed for violating law against political agitation
1949	forms the Convention People's Party
1950–51	is imprisoned during state of emergency
1951	becomes "leader of government business"
1952	becomes first prime minister of the Gold Coast
1957	Gold Coast gains independence as Ghana
1960	Nkrumah becomes president under republican constitution
1962	receives the Lenin Peace Prize; is target of assassination attempt
1964	decrees himself president for life; is target of second assassination attempt
1966	is deposed while visiting China
April 27, 1972	Kwame Nkrumah dies in Bucharest, Romania

Further Reading

Kellner, Douglas. *Kwame Nkrumah*. New York: Chelsea House, 1987. Biography in Chelsea's series on world leaders for young adult readers.

Nkrumah, Kwame. *Ghana: The Autobiography of Kwame Nkrumah*. New York: Thomas Nelson & Sons, 1957. Detailed autobiography recounting Nkrumah's life through Ghana's independence in 1957.

Owusu-Ansah, David, and Daniel Miles McFarland. *Historical Dictionary of Ghana*. 2d ed. Metuchen, N.J.: Scarecrow Press, 1995. Handbook to consult while reading about Nkrumah.

Rooney, David. *Kwame Nkrumah: The Political Kingdom in the Third World*. New York: St. Martin's Press, 1988. Full-scale biography of Nkrumah that attempts to place him in the wider perspective of modern African history.

Léopold Senghor with his son, Philippe, at the piano in 1962   (Archive Photos)

Léopold Senghor of Senegal

In the spring of 1940, German armies swept through Western Europe, pouring into France so fast that resistance collapsed almost immediately. Among the many French units the Germans captured was a regiment guarding a bridge near Vichy. When the Germans discovered that the defenders were mostly colonial troops, they separated the African soldiers, lined them up against a wall, and formed a firing squad to shoot them. Seconds away from dying, the Africans cried out: "Long live France! Long live Africa!" Suddenly, the Germans lowered their guns. A French officer had talked their commander out of committing the ghastly war crime.

None of the Africans who came so close to death that day would ever forget that experience. Among them was a Senegalese student named Léopold Senghor. He considered it a rebirth—after which he could face any danger without fear. That this was so, he later proved many times.

The path that Léopold Sédar Senghor followed to attain power in the French West Africa colony of Senegal was fundamentally different from those taken by Ghana's Kwame Nkrumah and other leaders in British colonial Africa. Not only did the French administer their colonies differently, Senegal itself occupied a unique place in French Africa.

When Senghor was born, on October 9, 1906, most of Senegal had been under French rule for only a few decades. However, parts of the colony had been administered by France since the late 18th century. The port of Dakar and three other cities—collectively known as the four communes —enjoyed a special relationship with France: Everyone born in these cities automatically became a French citizen. The communes contained many French-educated Africans who grew used to exercising the same political rights as French citizens in France. Since 1872 they had been electing deputies to represent them in the French National Assembly in Paris.

Through most of the 20th century French colonial policy stressed the principle of "assimilation." It was built on the notion that France and its colonies would eventually merge into a single greater France, and that the formerly colonized peoples would adopt the presumably superior French culture and become French themselves. After Senegal's Blaise Diagne became the first black African elected to the French assembly in 1914 (Senegal's earlier deputies had been white colonists), he outranked most of the white colonial officials in Africa, and he and his successors played integral roles in governing France itself. No other European colonial power had a philosophy comparable to France's. British-ruled Africans had no voice in the British government and scarcely had a voice in administrating their own colonies until well into the 20th century.

While France's colonial ideal in Senegal was assimilation, this did not carry over into the actual governing of the colony.

Most of Senegal was governed as a protectorate whose peoples were regarded as "subjects," not "citizens." Subjects had almost no political rights at all. Moreover, Senegal itself was part of the vastly larger French West Africa—which ranged from Senegal and Mauritania on the west coast to Niger in the east, and Senegal's interests were often considered secondary to those of the federation as whole. However, Senegal gained some advantages from having its own capital city, Dakar, serve as the federation capital.

By 1960 all the French West Africa colonies—Dahomey (now Benin), Guinea, Ivory Coast (Côte d'Ivoire), Mali, Mauritania, Niger, Senegal, and Upper Volta (now Burkina Faso)—would become independent republics through mostly peaceful and orderly transitions. Until the 1950s, however, Senegalese politics revolved around reconciling the differences between the communes and the protectorate, defining Senegal's relationship with France, and working out its relationships with other West African colonies.

Nothing about Senghor's birth and early years suggested that he would one day rule Senegal. His birthplace, the coastal village of Joal, was in the protectorate portion of Senegal, so he was not born a French citizen. Moreover, the ethnic group to which he belonged, the Serer, made up a small minority; the most numerous people were the Wolof. Finally, Senghor was raised as a Christian in a country whose population was more than 90 percent Muslim. In a part of the world where ethnic and religious affiliations have often played determinative roles in national politics, Senghor had almost everything going against him.

Senegal has limited natural resources and its prosperity —which has never been great—has rested largely on its agricultural crops, particularly peanuts (called groundnuts in Africa). Senghor's father was a moderately successful peanut grower and trader. However, he had several wives and more than two dozen children, so he would never be in a position to contribute much to his son's advancement. What Senghor eventually achieved, he earned largely on his own merits through hard work and perseverance.

Known as Sédar throughout his youth, Senghor spent his first seven years mostly in his mother's village and rarely saw his father. When he was seven, his mother placed him in a Roman Catholic school in Joal. Seven decades later he would receive the exalted honor of being elected to the French Academy. Academy members are famous for their distinguished mastery of the French language; however, when Senghor started school he did not speak a single word of French.

He learned quickly, however, and was advanced to the missionary school at nearby Ngazobil the following year—the same year that Diagne entered the French parliament. There he distinguished himself by winning all the school's academic prizes. He then attended a seminary in Dakar run by the Order of the Holy Spirit. By the time he graduated, he had become a devout Catholic and wanted to train for the priesthood. He was devastated when he was not recommended for clerical training—apparently because of the headmaster's personal antipathy toward him.

Senghor's academic career might have foundered at that point, but he was exceptionally lucky to join the tiny number of Africans admitted into the Lycée Van Vollenhoven, a government secondary school in Dakar. It had recently been created to give children of local French residents an education identical to what they would get in a public lycée in France. When Senghor graduated in 1928, he earned a distinction that made him legendary among the school's future African pupils: He won every single academic prize that the school offered.

The lycée's principal, recognizing Senghor's exceptional gifts, threatened to resign if the governor-general did not award Senghor a scholarship to study in France. The governor-general gave Senghor his scholarship—but on the condition that he serve the federation for 10 years after he returned home.

When Senghor arrived in Paris in late 1928, he found it wet, gray, and dreary, and did not take well to his classes at the Sorbonne. Happily for him, he switched to an elite secondary school, the Lycée Louis-le-grand, which had prepared many distinguished people for higher academic achievements. Over the next three years he flourished there and made close friends with students from around the empire who would later become government leaders in their own countries. Among them was future French president Georges Pompidou, who remained Senghor's lifelong friend.

After graduating from Louis-le-grand, Senghor set his sights on the difficult *agrégé* degree—roughly equivalent to an American Ph.D. He entered the Sorbonne to study literature in anticipation of becoming a teacher. As his work progressed, he encountered an unexpected obstacle: He could not take the *agrégé* examinations unless he was a French citizen, so he applied for naturalization. After becoming a French citizen in 1933, he had to serve in the military for a year; however, he got himself stationed close enough to Paris to continue his studies.

In August 1935, shortly after Senghor completed his military duty, he became the first African ever to pass the *agrégé* examinations. With the approval of French West Africa's governor-general, he accepted a teaching job at a lycée in the city of Tours, while continuing to study African languages and culture in Paris. He later described this period as his coming of age. Nearly 30 years old, he was teaching full-time, taking his academic work to a new level of maturity, and broadening his social and political horizons.

While at Louis-le-grand, Senghor had begun writing poetry, drawing mostly on memories of his African childhood

> We are complexed
> when we do not accept
> ourselves for what we
> are: as Arab-Berbers,
> as Negro-Africans, with
> our qualities as well as
> our faults . . .
>
> —Léopold Senghor

for themes. Contacts with black students and writers from other parts of the French Empire broadened his view of the world and encouraged him to think of himself more as a black person and not just an African. One of his most important friendships was with the West Indian intellectual Aimé Césaire, with whom he developed a philosopy that Césaire dubbed *négritude*, which explores the special nature of being black. Part of the essence of this philosophy is the belief that black people derive exceptional strength from their ability to feel and express emotion.

When Senghor made his first return visit to Senegal in 1932, he found his father in poor health and beset by financial problems. By the time of his second visit, in 1937, Senghor's father was dead, and his own ties with his homeland were weakening. He might have made his future as a scholar in France, had he not delivered a speech before colonial administrators and young Africans in Dakar during this visit. The speech marked the beginning of his public life. By challenging the negative assumptions of local elites about the potential of African education, he made a strong impression that would be remembered when he entered politics a decade later. Back in Paris afterward, he made another important public speech, this time to the distinguished International Congress on the Evolution of Peoples.

Senghor's budding academic career was interrupted by the onset of World War II. After Germany invaded Poland in September 1939, he was called to active duty by his infantry regiment. But France did not mobilize its forces, and the unit did not see action; however, by the following spring, the imminent danger of a German invasion prompted another call-up. This time Senghor had a brief taste of combat before his unit surrendered to the invaders. After narrowly escaping death at the hands of a German firing squad, Senghor became a prisoner of war. Over the next 18 months he was moved from camp to camp, but used the time well by writing poetry, reading, learning German, and teaching fellow Africans to read. By early 1942 France was fully under German control and Senghor's health was frail, so the Germans released him. He returned to Paris and resumed his academic work.

The end of the war in 1945 brought a rush of political changes to France. As a well-educated African in Paris, Senghor was invited to join a commission set up by the provisional French government to study how the colonies would be represented in the postwar government. His work on this committee helped make him one of the most respected African spokespersons in Paris. His reputation was further helped by the publication of his first full volume of poetry, *Chants d'Ombre* (Shadow Songs).

Still interested in African languages, Senghor returned to Senegal with a grant to study Wolof and Serer poetry. During this visit he consulted with the politician Lamine Guèye, Blaise Diagne's successor as Senegalese deputy to the French National Assembly. A new constituent assembly was forming in France to which Senegal was to send two deputies. Guèye wanted Senghor to run for one seat, while he ran for the other. Senghor had never thought of undertaking a political career, so he hesitated before finally agreeing to run. In the October 1945 election both men won, so Senghor again returned to France, this time as the political protégé of Guèye. In Paris he was invited to be one of the four colonial members of a special committee delegated to write a new national constitution.

The next few years were busy ones for Senghor. In 1946 he was elected to the reconstituted French National Assembly under the Fourth Republic, which was created by the new constitution. He also married Ginette Oboué, the daughter of Félix Oboué, the West Indian governor of French Equatorial Africa who had supported General Charles de Gaulle and the Free French during the war. In Paris he helped found a new black cultural journal, *Présence Africaine*, and he started his own Senegalese newspaper, *La Condition Humaine*.

Senghor began his political career under the guidance of Guèye, but after a few years he grew impatient with the lack of attention that Guèye's party was paying to African problems. In 1948 he broke from Guèye and formed a new party, Bloc Démocratique Sénégalais (BDS), which would be more dedicated to the interests of Senegal and West Africa.

After the war Africans in the rural regions of Senegal received the vote, and Senghor crisscrossed the country to build up support for the BDS. In countless villages he spoke before the citizens, impressing them with his eloquence, modesty, and courage in the face of occasional attacks by political rivals. He also established strong alliances with the leaders of Senegal's powerful Muslim brotherhoods, although he remained a devout Christian. At the next territorial elections, in 1951, Senghor's party pulled off a stunning upset. He and his running mate won both seats to the French National Assembly. With Guèye out of office, Senghor became Senegal's unchallenged political leader.

One of Senghor's fears about Senegal's future was the possibility that French West Africa would be "balkanized," that is, broken into its constituent states, each of them too small and weak ever to achieve anything. He wanted desperately to find ways of preserving some form of union among the West African colonies, but he never achieved anything lasting. He met several times with the Ivory Coast's Félix Houphouët-Boigny, the acknowledged leader of French West

Africa politicians, but they never came to any understanding on West African unity.

As Senghor continued to strengthen his leadership position within Senegal, world events were pushing France toward liberating its colonies. France faced violent anticolonial demonstrations in Madagascar; it was losing its war against Vietnamese nationalists in Indochina; and a major insurgency was developing in Algeria. The dream of a greater France incorporating its colonies was clearly not going to be realized.

Through these troubled years, Senghor himself played an important role in restructuring the French Empire, which was now being called the French Union. In 1955 Prime Minister Edgar Faure brought him into the French cabinet, and Senghor helped negotiate independence agreements with Tunisia and Morocco. Within Senegal Senghor was beginning to speak out in favor of "autonomy," but was not yet ready to demand independence.

One of Senghor's great strengths as a political leader was his ability to bring opponents into his camp. In 1956 he pulled together Senegal's four main political parties—including his own BDS—into a new party, the Bloc Populaire Sénégalais (BPS). Two years later he persuaded Lamine Guèye to merge his party into the BPS, which then became Union Progressiste Sénégalais (UPS). As the head of this party, Senghor directed virtually all political activity within Senegal.

By this time, events outside of West Africa were dictating the next step in France's relationship with its colonies. A French army mutiny in Algeria in 1958 brought down the Fourth Republic. Charles de Gaulle returned as president and soon invited the colonies to decide for themselves whether to remain in the French Union. In a referendum held throughout West Africa, members of each colony were given a simple choice: independence or union. Many Senegalese political leaders wanted immediate independence, but Senghor feared that the time was not right and that the terms of independence would be too costly. Following his lead, Senegal voted 98 percent in favor of remaining in the French Union. Senghor's wisdom in making this choice was quickly demonstrated by Guinea's example. After that country voted for independence, it was abruptly cut loose and left to find its own way, without preparation or assistance. Less than two years later Senegal and the other French West Africa colonies became independent on vastly more favorable terms.

Meanwhile, Senghor began working to prepare Senegal for independence. He was so anxious to create some kind of voluntary West African union that he was willing to sacrifice much of Senegal's sovereignty for the greater goal. However, the only other colony willing to join Senegal was the French Sudan. In 1959 Senegal and the French Sudan formed the Mali Federation, which took its named from the old Mali Empire, which had flourished in West Africa from the 13th to the 15th centuries.

In June 1960 the Mali Federation became independent, with the Sudanese leader Modibo Keita as president of the federation, Senghor as president of the National Assembly, and Mamadou Dia as prime minister and minister of defense. Only two months later, while he was vacationing in France, Senghor learned that Keita was planning to take complete control of the government and declare it a unitary state. Senghor immediately returned to Dakar and quickly, but calmly, took command of the situation. Keita and his associates were arrested and returned to the French Sudan, and Senghor proclaimed the end of the federation. In August Senegal adopted its own constitution, making it an independent republic (the Sudan also became independent, keeping the name Mali). Senghor was then officially elected president of the Republic of Senegal.

U.S. president John F. Kennedy greets Senghor on his arrival in Washington in April 1961, immediately after Senghor addressed the United Nations. (Archive Photos)

For the first time in many years, Senghor had no ties to the French government and he could focus his energies on Senegal. However, he left the day-to-day administration of the government to his close associate Mamadou Dia, the prime minister. This arrangement worked well for two years, but Senghor and Dia eventually split over economic policy. The precise sequence of events in late 1962 has never been established, but the outcome is clear. Senghor charged Dia with attempting to take over the government illegally and had him arrested and tried for treason. Sentenced to life in prison, Dia eventually served 12 years.

Meanwhile, Senghor surprised many observers by proving how tough he could be in a crisis. Unlike previous political crises he had weathered, this one could not be settled by a compromise, so he had to act quickly and decisively. With Dia out of the picture, he had the constitution revised to eliminate the office of prime minister and make his own office more powerful. He was reelected to the presidency unopposed.

Like many other African rulers, Senghor gradually became more authoritarian and out of touch with his people. However, he differed greatly from other rulers of his generation in avoiding violence and in adhering to constitutional principles—which, of course, changed as he had the constitution revised.

By the early 1970s the mood of the country was changing. There was considerable dissatisfaction with the lack of economic development, and there was growing resentment against Senghor for retaining a large number of French technical advisors at Senegal's expense. The government bureaucracy was bloated with the large numbers of people whom Senghor had won over with government jobs, and French companies were prospering within Senegal. Senghor's reputation as a man of the people was gone.

Finally, he began to acknowledge the need for political reform. In 1970 he reestablished the office of prime minister, to which he named Abdou Diouf, an able young technocrat. Several years later, Senghor reshuffled his cabinet to bring in younger ministers, freed political prisoners—including Dia —and allowed the formation of rival political parties. By the late 1970s Senegal was becoming one of the freest nations in Africa, but there was still considerable unrest because of hard economic conditions.

Despite his slipping popularity, Senghor was reelected president several times during the 1970s, and he might easily have followed the example of many other African leaders by trying to stay in office permanently. However, at the end of 1980 he did something that no other modern African ruler had done before: He voluntarily resigned, leaving the presidency to Diouf.

Senegal saw little economic progress during Senghor's two decades in power, but it had something that few other African nations enjoyed: a stable government that respected human rights and allowed relatively free and vigorous political debate. The year that Senghor left office Amnesty International, the international human rights watchdog organization, rated Senegal as having one of the best human rights records in the world.

Although Senghor was 75 years old when he resigned from politics, he enjoyed a long, busy, and rewarding retirement, devoting much of his time to his writing. After divorcing his first wife in 1956, he had married

[Senghor is] the living symbol of the possible synthesis of what appears irreconcilable: he is as African as he is European, as much a poet as a politician . . . as much a revolutionary as a traditionalist.

—Jacques Louis Hymans

a French woman, Colette Hubert, a year later. In his retirement he lived in both Senegal and France, gradually spending most of his time in Paris and at his wife's family home in Normandy.

In 1984 Senghor became the first black member of the French Academy, which recognized his distinguished contributions to literature, as well as his statesmanship. The following year France's Bibliothèque Nationale honored him with an exhibition of his work. In 1996 France and Senegal joined in celebrating Léopold Senghor's 90th birthday.

Chronology

October 9, 1906	Léopold Sédar Senghor is born in Joal, Senegal
1928	begins studies in Paris
1933	is naturalized as a French citizen
1935	passes *agrégation* examination
1935–39	teaches in Tours
1940–42	is a prisoner of war
1945	publishes first volume of poetry; is elected to French Constituent Assembly
1946	helps write constitution for France's Fourth Republic; is elected to French National Assembly; marries Ginette Oboué
1948	forms Bloc Démocratique Sénégalais
1955	serves as a member of French cabinet
1957	forms Senegalese government; marries Colette Hubert
1958	Senegal votes to stay in the French Union
1959	Senegal and French Sudan form Mali Federation

1960	Mali Federation becomes independent; Mali Federation dissolves; Senghor becomes president of independent Senegal
1981	retires from public office; is succeeded by Abdou Diouf
1984	is elected the first black member of the French Academy

Further Reading

Clark, Andrew F., and Lucie Colvin Phillips. *Historical Dictionary of Senegal*. Metuchen, N.J.: Scarecrow Press, 1994. Handy compilation of information on Senghor and Senegal.

Collins, Grace. *Man of Destiny: Léopold Senghor of Senegal*. Mount Airy, Md.: Sights Productions, 1997. Biography written for young readers.

Hymans, Jacques L. *Léopold Sédar Senghor: An Intellectual Biography*. Edinburgh, Scotland: Edinburgh University Press, 1971. Study of Senghor's life through his poetry and other writings.

Spleth, Janice. *Léopold Sédar Senghor*. Boston: Twayne Publishers, 1985. Survey of Senghor's published writings, which are discussed within the broader context of his life.

Vaillant, Janet G. *Black, French, and African: A Life of Léopold Sédar Senghor*. Cambridge, Mass.: Harvard University Press, 1990. Rich full-length biography, treating all dimensions of the multifaceted Senghor.

Julius K. Nyerere during the early 1960s, when he was president of the Republic of Tanganyika (Archive Photos)

Julius K. Nyerere of Tanzania

During the 1930s a young African attending Tanganyika's only government secondary school was surprised to learn that student prefects had special dining privileges, as well as disciplinary powers over fellow students. Denouncing such blatant inequalities as unacceptable in his impoverished country, he agitated to have these privileges taken away from the prefects. The success of his campaign was notable—not merely because of his courage in challenging colonial authority, but because he himself was one of the prefects whose privileges were ended.

People who knew the young Julius K. Nyerere in those days were not surprised by his behavior after he led Tanganyika to independence many years later. In contrast to almost every African ruler of his generation, Nyerere spurned the special privileges and trappings of power, while consistently championing economic and political equality for all Tanzanians. When he eventually retired, he would become one of Africa's few rulers to give up power voluntarily.

The vast East African nation of Tanzania sprang from the merger of Tanganyika and the coastal islands of Zanzibar. Zanzibar played an important role in Tanganyika's earlier history, but through most of the 20th century the two regions had few ties. One of the most important features of Tanganyika's earlier history was the division of its peoples into many separate societies. No powerful kingdoms ruled large regions, and no big ethnic groups dominated. It was a sharp contrast to the situations in countries such as Ethiopia, Kenya, and Zimbabwe.

Tanzania's modern boundaries were originally demarcated during the 1880s when Germany joined the European scramble for African territory and carved out Togo, Kamerun, South West Africa, and German East Africa. While a British-chartered company advanced into present-day Kenya and Uganda, a Germany company began developing German East Africa in what is now mainland Tanzania. In 1885 Germany declared a protectorate over part of Tanzania's coast, and it took over the company's administration of the territory five years later. Germany would also have seized Zanzibar, as well, had not Great Britain made that Arab-ruled state a protectorate in 1890.

Germany initially tried to develop its East African colony by forcing Africans to serve the needs of a growing settler population that was introducing modern agriculture. The Germans met such fierce resistance, however, that they eventually conceded that the colony's best chance for development lay in small-scale African agriculture. Germany struggled to find its way in East Africa, but nevertheless built up a system of roads and communications and developed a territorial administration that helped foster a sense of territorial identity among Africans.

Germany's budding African empire was abruptly ended by World War I (1914–18), during which German East Africa became the scene of some of the war's most intense fighting on African soil. By the end of the war Great Britain controlled German East Africa. Postwar European treaties stripped Germany of its colonies, but did not simply turn them over to the countries that had occupied them. Instead, the former German colonies became wards of the new League of Nations. The league, in turn, entrusted their administration to other European powers as mandate territories. In this way, the bulk of German East Africa was mandated to Great Britain, which already ruled neighboring Uganda, Kenya, and Zanzibar. It was renamed Tanganyika, after the magnificent inland lake that separated it from the Belgian Congo. (Rwanda and Burundi were mandated to Belgium.) As a mandate territory Tanganyika had a special international status that set it apart from other British colonies and played a role in its constitutional development.

Future president Julius Kambarage Nyerere happened to be born at a crucial moment in Tanganyika's political history. The exact date of his birth was not recorded, but it probably fell in March 1922—four months before the League of Nations formally approved the British mandate over German East Africa.

Nyerere was born into one of the smallest of Tanganyika's more than 100 ethnic groups: the Zanaki people, who comprised several small chiefdoms living on the eastern side of Lake Victoria in northern Tanganyika. Nyerere's father, Nyerere Burito (c. 1860–1942), was one of several chiefs recognized by the colonial administration, but he and his fellow chiefs were no better off than most of their impoverished subjects. Nyerere's mother, Mugaya, was one of Burito's 22 wives, who together produced 26 children.

Zanaki youths of Nyerere's generation expected little more from life than carrying on the subsistence farming practiced by their parents. From an early age, however,

Nyerere's intellect stood out so strongly he was sent to school at nearby Musoma. There he performed so well that he was admitted to the colony's only secondary school at Tabora, where he had his first encounters with Europeans.

At Tabora Nyerere again impressed his teachers and was encouraged to continue his education. In 1943 he entered East Africa's first institution of higher learning, Makerere University College in Uganda, where he earned a teaching certificate two years later. By then he had converted to Roman Catholicism, and he returned to Tabora to teach at a Catholic school. Encouraged by the White Fathers who ran that school, he then applied for a scholarship to attend Edinburgh University in Scotland in 1949. Even at that late date, he became the first Tanganyikan to attend a British university.

After earning a master's degree at Edinburgh, Nyerere returned to Tanganyika, married a woman named Maria Gabriel, and resumed his teaching career at another Roman Catholic school. He shocked many fellow Africans by building a traditional house with his own hands—an unheard-of task for an African university graduate.

After the end of World War II in 1945, the new United Nations (U.N.) had assumed responsibility for the mandate territories, which became U.N. Trust Territories. Before the war Tanganyika had seen little political or economic development, so the new U.N. Trusteeship Council began pressuring Britain to do more. Britain began building more schools and investing more in agriculture, but the pace of these advances was slow. Their main effect was to encourage Tanganyikans to become more politically assertive. There was widespread discontent among farmers, who comprised 95 percent of the population. They were particularly concerned about forced agricultural schemes and unfair taxation and feared having their land taken away. There were no nationwide political organizations at that time and Africans had little direct voice in the government. Rising political tensions made the situation ripe for a national leader.

As so often happened to colonial Africans educated abroad, Nyerere's experiences at Makerere and Edinburgh opened his eyes to the world and triggered his serious interest in politics. Acutely aware of Tanganyika's low level of development, he wanted to devote himself to uplifting the country as a whole. Since his Makerere days he had been a member of the Tanganyika African Association (TAA), a fraternal organization that the British administration had created in 1929 for civil servants. In 1953 he was elected president of the TAA.

Since the TAA was not a true political organization, Nyerere began working to create one. He traveled widely throughout the country in a battered Land Rover, drumming up interest in a new political party. In 1954 he helped pull together TAA branches and affiliates to launch the Tanganyika Africa National Union (TANU). TANU differed from the TAA in being expressly dedicated to African political advancement. The date of its formation—July 7—later became a national holiday, called *Saba Saba*—Swahili for "seven seven," after the seventh day of the seventh month.

Over the next seven years TANU experienced a level of unity and success with few parallels in colonial African nationalist movements. The reasons lay in both Tanganyika's unique history and Nyerere's astute leadership. The absence of dominant ethnic groups within Tanganyika prevented ethnic rivalries, and the movement benefited from an unusual degree of linguistic unity. Tanganyikans spoke dozens of languages, but many people also spoke Swahili, a widely used coastal language. The inland trade routes emanating from Zanzibar during the 19th century helped spread the language, as did expansion of the German colonial administration in the early 20th century.

Swahili was an ideal tool for unifying Tanganyika politically. It was a native African language that was widely understood and not identified with any one ethnic group. Nyerere made a special effort to promote Swahili as a national language. In later years he published Swahili translations of William Shakespeare's plays.

In 1954 Nyerere was briefly appointed to a seat on Tanganyika's Legislative Council (Legco), but had little chance to accomplish anything. By the following year he was spending more time on his political work than his teaching, so he quit his job. Frustrated with the colonial administration's unsatisfactory progress toward majority rule, he decided to take the colony's case to a higher authority, the United Nations—an option not open to nationalists in most other African colonies. What he particularly wanted was a U.N. declaration that Tanganyika's future government would be primarily African. However, he soon understood that the U.N. would not act to assure independence for Tanganyika, so he determined to concentrate on strengthening TANU.

After World War II British policy in Tanganyika fostered a form of multiracialism that gave equal political representation to Africans, Europeans, and Asians, despite the overwhelming numerical superiority of Africans. Nyerere consistently advocated nonracialism (representation without regard for race, ensuring majority rule) and spoke out fiercely against the government. In an apparent attempt to silence Nyerere's criticisms by bringing him into the government, the administration again made him a member of Legco in 1957. However, he merely used his Legco seat to continue his campaign for substantive political change; when he became disgusted with the lack of political progress, he resigned. The following year the government tried to silence him by convicting him of libel for an article in a TANU newspaper it claimed he had written.

In 1958 Nyerere faced his first major leadership crisis. The government scheduled legislative elections under a plan that would elect equal numbers of Africans, Asians, and Europeans to Legco. All candidates were to be elected on a common voters' roll, but restrictions on voting eligibility severely limited the number of African voters. Although Nyerere liked the scheme no better than other TANU leaders, he argued against boycotting the elections. TANU's sweep of the ensuing elections vindicated his decision and demonstrated that the multiracial formula was not acceptable.

The following year Britain brought in a new governor, R. G. Turnbull, who favored African majority rule. Political change then came at an accelerated pace. After Turnbull ordered new elections in 1960 that would permit an outright African legislative majority, TANU achieved a sweeping victory at the polls. In October Tanganyika was granted internal self-government and Nyerere became chief minister.

Like Ghana's Kwame Nkrumah, Nyerere favored the eventual union of Africa under one government. Being a pragmatist, he realized that continental unification must develop in stages and hoped to begin the process by unifying East Africa. As Tanganyika moved closer to winning its freedom, he offered to delay its full independence until Uganda and Kenya were also ready for self-government. This did not come about, however, and Tanganyika became independent on December 9, 1961, with Nyerere as its first prime minister.

Although Tanganyika achieved its independence without violence and almost no ethnic, racial, or religious conflict, independence brought a host of new problems. The country immediately ranked as one of the world's poorest, and it had too few educated people to run its government offices and institutions without outside help. Nyerere adopted as a national motto the Swahili phrase *uhuru na kazi*, "freedom

During the first year of Tanganyikan independence Nyerere and his close ally, Rashidi Kawawa, promoted the philosophy of self-help by personally engaging in physical labor in a housing project. (Archive Photos)

and work," but the public response was meager—perhaps because of the relatively easy achievement of independence.

In early 1962 Nyerere shocked Tanganyika and the world by resigning his premiership in order to focus on rebuilding TANU. During his time out of power, Tanganyika's constitution was revised to replace the prime minister's position with an executive president and make the country a republic. In December Nyerere ran for president and was elected with a 97 percent majority. During the year that followed he articulated his philosophy of democratic socialism in a book titled *Democracy and the Party*.

The year 1964 brought a new set of challenges. At the end of 1963 Britain had granted independence to Zanzibar under the islands' traditional Arab government. A popular African uprising led by a Ugandan quickly overthrew the Arab government; then the coup leaders themselves were soon overthrown. Events in Zanzibar triggered army mutinies in Tanganyika, Kenya, and Uganda in January 1964. The uprising in Tanganyika was dangerous enough to force Nyerere to flee from Dar es Salaam, but he did not hesitate to call in British troops to help put the mutiny down.

Meanwhile, the new rulers in Zanzibar looked to Tanganyika for support. In late April Nyerere again shocked the world by announcing that Tanganyika and Zanzibar would merge. It was the first instance of a voluntary union between two sovereign African nations that would endure for any length of time. In late October the union was formalized when the new country officially became the United Republic of Tanzania. However, despite the formal trappings of unity, Zanzibar long afterward remained largely autonomous of the mainland and Nyerere had little say in its internal affairs.

In 1965 Nyerere pushed his political philosophy closer to realization by overseeing the transformation of the nation into a one-party state under TANU. Believing that Western two-party democracy would be wasteful and potentially disruptive in his own country, he favored a one-party system in which, he argued, open debate would be maintained and true democracy would exist. In the country's first one-party elections in September, his theory was vindicated when voters turned large numbers of incumbent politicians out of office. A major reason for voter dissatisfaction with elected officials was resentment against their high incomes and special privileges.

No other African head of state has set such high standards for his countrymen, for Africa or, for that matter, for all mankind . . .

—John Darnton,
New York Times

One of the most impressive characteristics of Nyerere's leadership was his consistent adherence to moral principles, which he was willing to make sacrifices to support. In late 1965, for example, after the white settler regime ruling Southern Rhodesia (now Zimbabwe) unilaterally declared independence, Nyerere was upset by Britain's failure to force the illegal regime into line. Although Tanzania was about to receive a desperately needed development loan from Britain, Nyerere broke diplomatic relations with Britain to protest its Rhodesian policy. Two years later he opposed the stance of almost every African nation by recognizing the independence of Nigeria's seceding region, Biafra, on moral grounds.

Within Tanzania Nyerere was willing to make even greater sacrifices in the interest of democratic principles. In early February 1967 he issued a declaration from Arusha that outlined his basic Socialist philosophy and called for major policy changes. The declaration required all party leaders—including Nyerere himself—to divest themselves of private sources of income and take pay cuts. It also proposed concentrating peasant farmers into community (*ujamaa*) villages and called for the nationalization of banks and many industries.

The Arusha Declaration, as it became known, defined the course of Tanzanian socialism over the next two decades. The policy's basic thrust was to focus on developing the country from the grassroots levels and to avoid dependence on outside aid. Nyerere personally articulated this philosophy in his speeches and writings and was not above going out to work with his hands among ordinary citizens to make his point. However, most of his economic policies produced little result, and Tanzania remained one of Africa's major recipients of foreign aid.

Many would argue that the failure of Nyerere's brand of socialism was due most to intractable problems of poverty and external conditions, such as foreign oil embargoes. Whatever the verdict on his economic policies, he continued to win international recognition for his moral leadership in a continent whose leaders were becoming known increasingly for their corruption, brutality, and authoritarianism. Nyerere consistently spoke out strongly against human rights abuses. In 1978 he braved the displeasure of the Organization of African Unity by sending Tanzanian troops into Uganda to topple the brutal dictatorship of Idi Amin.

When Nyerere was elected to another five-year term as president in 1980, he announced it would be his last. In November 1985 he carried out this promise by quietly stepping down and allowing newly elected Ali Hassan Mwinyi to succeed him as president. Europeans and Americans used to peaceful political transitions can scarcely appreciate what a significant event Nyerere's voluntary departure from power was in the African context. Since the early 1960s, all but a handful of the African leaders who have left office have done so because they have died, been driven out, or been killed.

In an effort to bring Zanzibar and mainland Tanzania closer together in 1977 TANU was merged with the leading Zanzibari political organization, the Afro-Shirazi Party. The combined organization was called Chama Cha Mapinduzi (CCM)

The Tanzanian experiment offers good evidence that saints do not really make very good presidents.

—Stanley Meisler

—Swahili for "Party of Revolution." Nyerere was chairman of the CCM on its founding, and he retained that position after retiring from the government in 1985. He retired from that position, too, five years later, but continued to speak out publicly when he was displeased with the direction that the government was taking.

Chronology

March 1922	Julius Kambarage Nyerere is born in Butiama, Tanganyika
1943–45	earns teaching certificate at Makerere
1946–49	teaches in Tabora
1949–52	attends Edinburgh University
1953	is elected president of the Tanganyika African Association
1954	serves on Legislative Council; founds Tanganyika African National Union
1957	serves on Legislative Council again
1960	becomes chief minister after TANU sweeps general elections
1961	becomes prime minister of independent Tanganyika
1962	resigns premiership to reorganize TANU; is elected president when Tanganyika becomes a republic
1964	Tanganyika and Zanzibar merge to become the United Republic of Tanzania
1967	Nyerere issues the Arusha Declaration; proclaims birth of East African Community
1975	is reelected president unopposed

1977	becomes chairman of Chama Cha Mapinduzi, which merges TANU and Afro-Shirazi Party
1978	sends troops against Uganda's Idi Amin
1980	is reelected president
1984–85	serves as chairman of Organization of African Unity
1985	retires from presidency and is succeeded by Ali Hassan Mwinyi
1990	retires from chairmanship of CCM

Further Reading

Du Bois, Shirley Graham. *Julius K. Nyerere: Teacher of Africa.* New York: Julian Messner, 1975. Biography for young adult readers.

Kurtz, Laura S. *Historical Dictionary of Tanzania.* Metuchen, N.J.: Scarecrow Press, 1978. Useful reference for people and places in Nyerere's life.

Legum, Colin, ed. *Mwalimu: The Influence of Nyerere.* Trenton, N.J.: African World Press, 1995. Essays assessing Nyerere's legacy a decade after his retirement from public office.

Smith, William Edgett. *We Must Run While They Walk: A Portrait of Africa's Julius Nyerere.* New York: Random House, 1971. Warmly sympathetic biography of Nyerere written for a general audience.

Jomo Kenyatta (left) with Ugandan premier Milton Obote, during an East African summit conference to discuss a political crisis in the Congo (later Zaire) (Archive Photos)

Jomo Kenyatta of Kenya

In mid-1936 a mostly black crowd quietly awaited a train at London's Waterloo Station. Its mood was somber. At that moment Italian armies were overrunning Ethiopia, the only African kingdom that had escaped colonialism. Ethiopia's conquest was a disaster to black people everywhere; now its emperor was arriving to begin what might become a permanent exile. After his train pulled into the station, Emperor Haile Selassie stepped out and acknowledged the crowd's welcome. Nothing in his dignified bearing invited familiarity, but a bearded man broke through a cordon, rushed up, and warmly embraced him.

That man, whose affection for the emperor outweighed his respect for protocol, was an impoverished student from British Kenya, a colony where the possibility of African government seemed more remote than Haile Selassie's own return to power. Yet Haile Selassie *would* return to Ethiopia; and years later he would visit Kenya as a guest of its first president—Jomo Kenyatta, the student who had embraced him in London.

The modern nation of Kenya began as a colony whose creation was almost an afterthought. When the British pushed into East Africa during the late 19th century, Kenya interested them only as an overland route to the colony they were building in Uganda. So ignorant were they of Kenya that its most numerous people, the Kikuyu of the central highlands, were unknown to them until 1883. A geologist who met the Kikuyu that year reported merely that they were a troublesome and intractable people. Their fearsome reputation and the land's evident lack of wealth did little to attract Europeans to their country.

Everything changed during the 1890s, when the Imperial British East Africa Company began preparing to cut a railroad through Kenya to connect Uganda with Mombasa on the coast. This intrusion turned the Kikuyu world upside down. In 1895 the British imperial government took over the company's ventures and declared Kenya a protectorate—officially the British East Africa Protectorate. As work on the railroad began in earnest, the British discovered that the Kikuyu homeland had a pleasant climate and fertile land that made it an attractive region to colonize. Growing numbers of British settlers soon arrived to stake out vast farms, and towns sprang up to serve new commercial needs.

> Gikuyu country was never wholly conquered . . . the people were put under the ruthless domination of European imperialism through the insidious trickery of hypocritical treaties.
>
> —Jomo Kenyatta

Some time during this period a Kikuyu boy named Kamau was born on the Ngenda Ridge, about 30 miles north of where the city Nairobi would later rise. Kamau was the first son of a man named Muigai and his wife, Wambui, who led typical Kikuyu lives raising crops and keeping sheep and goats. The date of Kamau's birth was not recorded, and he would go through life ever uncertain of his age. (Connections between events in his life and datable events have produced estimates of his birthdate ranging from 1890 to 1897.) As Kamau grew older he would change his name several times, but it would not be until 1938 that the world would know him as Jomo Kenyatta.

Kenyatta's life provides an interesting contrast to that of Ethiopia's Emperor Haile Selassie, who was born around the same time about 800 miles to the north. Whereas Haile Selassie was born into an aristocratic family in an independent Christian kingdom, Kenyatta was born into a decentralized egalitarian society that would soon fall under alien rule. The Kikuyu people governed themselves through extended family units that recognized a common culture and law; they worked out disputes through councils and consultations.

Kenyatta spent his early years like many African boys, herding flocks and learning social customs from his elders. His life grew much harder, however, after his father died while he was still young. Following Kikuyu practice, his mother then married his father's brother, Ngengi, who became responsible for raising his nephew. Soon after bearing Ngengi a son, his mother, too, died, leaving Kenyatta dependent on his severe uncle.

Some time during his youth Kenyatta encountered Scottish missionaries. In 1909 he went off on his own to enroll in their mission school at Thogoto. There he learned to read, write, and speak English, and he completed enough technical training to apprentice as a carpenter when he left in 1912. Meanwhile, he took a fancy to English names and began calling himself Johnstone Kamau. Although he converted to

Christianity, he underwent the traditional Kikuyu initiation and circumcision rites in 1913, a year before he was baptized into the Presbyterian Church.

The coming of World War I in 1914 suddenly made Kenya's southern neighbor, German East Africa (later Tanganyika), enemy territory, and the British protectorate mobilized for war. Most of its male settlers enlisted to fight, and Africans were pulled into service as carriers in the rugged campaigns into German territory. Thousands of Kikuyu were among the many Africans who died—mostly from disease —during the war. Afterward, European settlers who served in the war were liberally rewarded, but African veterans received nothing. Kenyatta himself evaded military service by living with a rural Masai family through the latter part of the war, but one of his brothers disappeared while serving in the carrier corps. In later years Kenyatta made the bitterness that African servicemen felt after the war an issue in his campaigns against the colonial government.

In 1920 the British East African Protectorate was reorganized as Kenya Colony. That same year Kenyatta married the first of four wives, Grace Wahu, who bore his first son in November. He also moved to Nairobi, where he landed an excellent job with the municipal waterworks as a stores clerk and meter reader. This job's prestige and salary enabled him to dress well, own a motorbike, and earn a reputation as a dandy. Possessing an outgoing personality, he enjoyed drawing attention to himself—a trait he retained throughout his life.

Nothing resembling Western political activity existed in Kenya before the British arrived, and after they began developing the colony they strove to discourage Africans from expecting to participate in its government. As the settlers increased their representation in the Legislative Council (Legco), they wanted complete control of the government —as Southern Rhodesian settlers achieved in 1923.

Shortly after Kenyatta settled in Nairobi, he joined a new political group—the East African Association. After the government outlawed this group, he joined its successor, the Kikuyu Central Association (KCA) in 1924. Questions about land distribution were becoming a major issue among the Kikuyu, many of whom had been displaced by British settlers. By 1928 Kenyatta was the KCA's general secretary and editor of its newsletter. While writing for this newsletter he again changed his name, to Johnstone Kenyatta. That same year he testified on the land question for the KCA before the Hilton Young Commission—the first of several government investigations into the issue. In early 1929 the KCA sent him to London to represent it before the Colonial Office.

Although Kenyatta's trip lasted a year and a half, he had trouble getting the attention of the Colonial Office and accomplished relatively little. Nevertheless, his status as one of the first Kikuyu to visit Britain enhanced his prestige at home, and the trip opened his eyes to the full strength of the Western world. He also worked in a visit to the new Soviet Union. Little is known about that episode, except that he came away with a favorable impression of communism.

When Kenyatta returned home in September 1930, the Kenya Colony was embroiled in a controversy over the Kikuyu custom of female circumcision. European missionaries and medical professionals regarded the practice as abhorrent and dangerous and wanted it outlawed. The dispute escalated into a major test of strength between the Kikuyu and the government and aggravated existing discontent over the land question. Meanwhile, as this issue was debated, a British parliamentary committee was preparing a new study of the Kenya land question, so the KCA again sent Kenyatta to England to represent it. He reached London in May 1931.

This time Kenyatta remained in Europe for 15 years. The experience would transform him and help elevate him to the leading position in Kenya's nationalist movement. When he finally returned to Kenya he would be largely free of the narrow focus that characterized many nationalist leaders. However, while he moved easily in European circles, he would never measure himself by European standards.

Kenyatta again did what he could in England to advance the KCA's interests: He met with government officials, testified on behalf of the Kikuyu whenever possible, and wrote letters and articles for British newspapers and Socialist publications denouncing British policies in Kenya. Meanwhile, he got to know the British well and enjoy himself. He worked when he had to—often as a language tutor—but never hesitated to accept hospitality when it was offered or to take advantage of soft-hearted landladies. He also spent considerable time outside of Britain and saw much of Europe. In late 1932 he went to Germany and became a friend of the West Indian Socialist George Padmore. Just before Adolf Hitler's Nazi Party came to power, he and Padmore continued on to Moscow, where Padmore had strong ties with the Communist International.

Little is known about Kenyatta's ensuing year in Russia. He is believed to have studied at the University of Moscow, but details are sparse. Since his earlier visit, the Soviet Union's economic and political situation had deteriorated badly, and he appears to have come away this time with a less favorable impression of communism. Nevertheless, in later years his British enemies would cite his time in Moscow and the fact that he wrote for Socialist papers to denounce him as a Communist and dangerous radical.

After Kenyatta returned to London in the fall of 1933, he settled down to the life of a struggling foreign student. The following year he had a bit part in Alexander Korda's film *Sanders of the River*, about a traditional African ruler's coming to terms with British colonialism. While working on that film, he became a friend of its star, the African-American singer Paul Robeson. During this period he also met other

Africans and black people from around the world, and he came to realize the limitations of his education. To correct this deficiency he enrolled in an anthropology program at the London School of Economics under the distinguished Bronsilaw Malinowski.

While working under Malinowski he wrote papers on the Kikuyu that he later assembled in a book, *Facing Mount Kenya* (1938). This work was at once an authentic examination of Kikuyu culture and a powerful argument against British imperialism. *Facing Mount Kenya* extolled African culture as inherently superior and cataloged ways in which the British were destroying it. The book had a meager sale on its initial publication but would later help to give Kenyatta the image of an articulate intellectual; it would also be recognized as a classic work of anthropology. To give the cover of his book an authentic African look, Kenyatta had himself photographed wearing animal skins; meditatively fingering the tip of a spear. When he published the book he invented a new name for himself: Jomo.

Around this same time Kenyatta became politically active alongside figures such as Padmore and Trinidad's C. L. R. James, who worked to unite the interests of the world's black peoples through the pan-African movement. As European tensions mounted in the late 1930s, this group planned to relocate to Norway for safety, but the outbreak of World War II in September 1939 closed that avenue of escape, effectively stranding Kenyatta in Britain. He then spent most of the war

[Kenyatta] was one of Dr. Malinowski's brightest pupils . . . A showman to his finger tips; jovial, a good companion, shrewd, fluent, quick, devious, subtle, flesh pot loving . . .

—fellow student Elspeth Huxley

Kenyatta had himself photographed in animal skins to illustrate his book Facing Mount Kenya *while he was living in London. He deliberately made his pose provocative by touching the tip of a spear (which he and a friend had carved from a single piece of wood).* (Archive Photos)

years in West Sussex, where he adapted to local English life and earned money doing farmwork.

Although Kenyatta was still married to Grace Wahu, he married an English woman named Edna Grace Clarke in May 1942. This marriage produced a son, Peter Magana, the following year, but neither Edna nor Peter would return with Kenyatta to Kenya. Before going home, Kenyatta helped organize the Fifth Pan-African Congress, held in Manchester in October 1945. Among the participants with whom he worked was Kwame Nkrumah, who would lead Ghana to independence a dozen years later. Meanwhile, Kenyatta finally returned to Kenya in September 1946. Except for a brief visit to England for a prime ministers' conference in 1964, he would never again leave Africa.

At home Kenyatta became the principal of an independent teacher's college started by his Kikuyu friend Peter Koinange. In June 1947 he was elected president of the new Kenya African Union (KAU), which had formed during his absence after the KCA had been banned. This moment may be considered the start of Kenya's modern nationalist movement, as Kenyatta worked to transform KAU into a truly national body that represented all Kenyans.

One of the chief obstacles that the nationalist movement faced was the political power of the white settlers; although their numbers were comparatively small, their wealth and political connections gave them tremendous political influence. To them, Kenyatta was the devil incarnate—a dangerous agitator with Communist ties who was dedicated to driving Europeans out of Kenya. The settlers did everything they could to discredit him while pushing their own plan for eventual independence under a white settler government.

A forceful speaker with a knack for addressing Africans in their own idiom, Kenyatta spent several years touring the country, attracting huge crowds to meetings at which he called for unity in the struggle for African rights. During this same period, a highly secret Kikuyu movement was developing that became known as Mau Mau. Following a Kikuyu tradition of oath-making rituals, members of this movement persuaded thousands of Kikuyu to swear solemn oaths to fight for Kikuyu rights. Those who refused were often killed—usually savagely. Some white settlers were also victims of grisly murders, and rumors circulated that Mau Mau members swore to kill all Europeans. Quite naturally, the government and settler community grew alarmed. In August 1950 the government outlawed what it called the "Mau Mau Association"; two years later it declared a state of emergency.

Even decades later the Mau Mau movement would not be fully understood, nor would the question of whether Kenyatta himself was connected with the movement be fully answered. Hard evidence linking Kenyatta to Mau Mau is almost nonexistent. Kenyatta had no known history of violent behavior and he himself consistently spoke out against the movement during its peak years. If anything, Mau Mau may have been motivated partly by the resentment of Kikuyu over Kenyatta's efforts to build a nontribal nationalist movement. Mau Mau was essentially a Kikuyu civil war (more than 1,800 Kikuyu are believed to have been killed by Mau Mau members, compared to less than three dozen Europeans).

Kenyatta's position as the most prominent Kikuyu opponent of the government and his reputation for radicalism made him a natural scapegoat of efforts to suppress Mau Mau. In October 1952 he was arrested and charged with leading a rebellion. In his ensuing trial, the government dredged up every questionable aspect of his past to discredit him. However, the only witness who actually linked Kenyatta to Mau Mau later recanted his testimony and was himself convicted of perjury. The weakness of the government's case did not, however, stop a British judge from finding Kenyatta guilty and sentencing him to seven years at hard labor. Several months later the government banned KAU.

Kenyatta got fine legal support from a prominent British barrister, but all attempts to appeal his conviction were dismissed. He was sent to a specially built prison encampment at Lokitaung, near Lake Rudolf in Kenya's restricted Northern Frontier District. A stiflingly hot, arid, and barren encampment in a desolate area, Lokitaung scarcely needed guards or fences to keep prisoners from escaping. Kenyatta was sentenced to hard labor, but because of his age—he may then have been over 60—he was required only to be the prison cook.

While in prison Kenyatta could correspond with relatives, but had no visitors and almost no news from outside. In addition, his health was threatened by the harsh climate and bad diet. He completed his prison sentence in April 1959, only to be moved to Lodwar—an even hotter village to the south of Lokitaung—to serve two more years under restriction. Kenyatta enjoyed more freedom at Lodwar but was still largely cut off from political developments in the colony.

During his long confinement much had happened. The government did not officially end the emergency until 1960, but the last Mau Mau murder occurred in early 1955. Two years later the first Africans were elected to Legco and it was becoming clear that the British government would insist that Africans, not settlers, lead Kenya into independence. In Kenyatta's absence, other Africans moved to the forefront of the nationalist movement, but his name was not forgotten.

With restrictions on political associations lifted, the Kenya African National Union (KANU) was formed in early 1960 to carry on KAU's program for a strong central government under majority rule. In May KANU's officers nominated Kenyatta as their president, but the governor—who regarded Kenyatta as personally responsible for Mau Mau —refused to allow him to participate in politics. From that point independence issues became inextricably tied to calls for Kenyatta's freedom. Early the following year KANU swept the first general elections, defeating its main rival, the Kenya African Democratic Union (KADU), a largely non-Kikuyu body that favored decentralized government.

In August 1961 Kenyatta was finally allowed to return home and be fully free. Events then moved quickly for him. In October he accepted KANU's presidency; three months later he entered Legco. In April 1962 he accepted a cabinet appointment. Meanwhile, he resumed campaigning, this time to prepare Africans for independence at the end of 1963. After KANU swept the general elections of May 1963, Kenyatta was invited to form a government as prime minister. On December 12 he presided over Kenya's independence ceremonies.

Although Kenyatta's popularity was unrivaled in the days leading to Kenya's independence, many—including some of his supporters—had reservations about his ability to lead the country. He had had no real experience in government and had long been out of touch with events, and many people thought he was becoming senile. However, he soon emerged as such a strong and decisive leader that even the white settlers who had long despised him would come to regard him as the key to Kenya's future.

Despite Kenyatta's past connections with Socialists and Communists, he was essentially a practical leader who stressed common human rights and national unity. Though he had built his political career in mainly Kikuyu organizations, his strongest contribution to Kenya was his insistence on national unity. Moreover, despite his ill treatment by the colonial government, he never complained or called for recriminations. Instead, he appealed to Kenyans to forget the wrongs of the past and work together for the future. His watchword *Harambee!* ("let us all pull together") became a national motto.

As prime minister, Kenyatta appointed a strong cabinet, representing all sections of the population including the settlers, and proved to be a master at balancing rival forces. A year after independence, parliament revised the constitution to make Kenya a republic. On December 12, 1964, Kenyatta became the nation's first executive president. Under a later constitution he was reelected to that office in 1970 and 1974. Meanwhile, he gradually strengthened the office of the presidency, while overseeing the steady growth of Kenya's economy.

After Kenyatta's death on August 22, 1978, he was succeeded as president by Daniel arap Moi, whom he had appointed vice president 11 years earlier.

Chronology

1890s	Jomo Kenyatta is born Kamau at Ngenda
1895	Great Britain declares protectorate over Kenya
1909	Kenyatta enrolls in Scottish mission school
1914	is baptized as Johnstone Kamau
1920	marries first wife, Grace Wahu; British East Africa becomes Kenya Colony
1922–28	Kenyatta begins political activity while working for Nairobi municipal water company; becomes general secretary of Kikuyu Central Association (KCA); adopts name Johnstone Kenyatta
1929–30	represents the KCA in England; visits Russia
1931–46	returns to England; stays in Europe 15 years

1938	publishes *Facing Mount Kenya*; adopts the name Jomo
1942	marries Edna Grace Clarke
1945	helps organize Fifth Pan-African Congress in Manchester
1946	returns to Kenya
1947	runs independent teacher's college; is elected president of KAU
1950–60	Kenya government declares state of emergency during Mau Mau disturbances
1953–61	Kenyatta is imprisoned for inciting rebellion
1961	accepts presidency of KANU
1962	enters Legco and becomes a cabinet minister
1963	forms a government after KANU sweeps elections; becomes prime minister as Kenya gains independence
1964	becomes president under republican constitution
August 22, 1978	Jomo Kenyatta dies in Mombasa and is succeeded as president by Daniel arap Moi

Further Reading

Abrahams, Peter. *A Wreath for Udomo*. London: Faber and Faber, 1965. Novel about an African, modeled on Kenyatta, leading his nation to independence, by a South African who knew Kenyatta during the 1940s.

Cuthbert, Valerie. *Jomo Kenyatta: The Burning Spear*. Harlow, England: Longman, 1982. Brief biography written for British schoolchildren.

Kenyatta, Jomo. *Facing Mount Kenya: The Tribal Life of the Gikuyu*. London: Secker and Warburg, 1938. Kenyatta's partly autobiographical book on Kikuyu culture is a key to understanding him.

———. *Suffering Without Bitterness: The Founding of the Kenya Nation*. Nairobi: East African Publishing House, 1968. Kenyatta's official biography.

Murray-Brown, Jeremy. *Kenyatta*. 2d ed. London: George Allen & Unwin, 1979. Sympathetic and readable treatment of Kenyatta's life.

Wepman, Dennis. *Jomo Kenyatta*. New York: Chelsea House, 1989. Biography for young readers emphasizing Kenyatta's early years.

Robert Mugabe while attending a U.N. conference on decolonization held in Mozambique in 1977 (Archive Photos)

Robert Mugabe of Zimbabwe

During the early 1940s a young Southern Rhodesian teacher was outraged when the superintendent of his school deducted an unexpected fee from his pay. Many Africans in his position would have accepted the blow quietly. His country had been colonized to serve European settlers, whose authority Africans were expected never to challenge. This teacher, however, would not accept injustice without a fight—which is precisely what he offered his white superintendent. No blows were exchanged, but the teacher got his money back. It would not be the last time he was prepared to fight for his rights.

His superintendent, Garfield Todd, also learned something from the incident. A decade later, when he became Southern Rhodesia's prime minister, he wrecked his career by standing up for African rights. He was finally vindicated in 1980, when Rhodesia became Zimbabwe. Todd was then appointed a senator by the nation's first new prime minister—the teacher who had once defied him, Robert Mugabe.

Among tropical Africa's many countries, Zimbabwe's colonial experience was unique. In large part this was due to its nearness to South Africa, from which its first colonizers came. During the early 1890s the British South Africa Company—directed by South African industrialist and politician Cecil Rhodes—occupied Zimbabwe. After winning two wars of conquest, the company started exploiting Zimbabwe's mineral riches, while encouraging white settlement from South Africa, Britain, and elsewhere. After several name changes, the new colony was called Southern Rhodesia, after its founder. (Its northern neighbor, Northern Rhodesia, was also created by Rhodes's company.)

In September 1923 the British government took over Southern Rhodesia. Although the new Crown Colony had only 35,000 European settlers—less than 5 percent the number of Africans (a proportion that never significantly increased)—Britain granted the settlers self-government in October. A white prime minister then took office, and the settlers began electing representatives to the new Legislative Assembly early the following year. Before all this happened, Britain offered the settlers the option to join South Africa, but they voted to stay separate, hoping one day to have their own fully independent white-ruled country.

British governors remained Southern Rhodesia's nominal heads of state, and Britain reserved the right to overrule certain kinds of legislation, but it never actually did so. Technically everyone in the colony had the right to vote, but the eligibility rules disqualified so many African voters that the government remained almost entirely white into the 1960s. In purely internal affairs, it was virtually independent —a situation without parallel in tropical Africa. What prevented Southern Rhodesia from simply going its own way was the smallness of its European population and Britain's control over its external affairs.

After the end of World War II in 1945, two major developments transformed Southern Rhodesia's future. The first was a large increase in European immigration. By the mid-1960s European residents numbered a quarter of a million people—enough for them to control the national economy, government, military, and police. The second was Britain's postwar effort to join Southern Rhodesia, Northern Rhodesia, and nearby Nyasaland in a federation designed to accelerate the economic development of all three territories. To many white Southern Rhodesians, formation of the Federation of Rhodesia and Nyasaland (usually called the Central African Federation) in 1953 presented an opportunity to create a new country that would rival South Africa in size. During the 10 years the federation lasted, white Southern Rhodesians dominated it. The federation failed primarily because Britain was pledged to advance the political rights of Africans in all three territories, and black Northern Rhodesians and Nyasalanders feared domination by white Southern Rhodesians.

After the federation officially expired at the end of 1963, Nyasaland became independent as Malawi and Northern Rhodesia as Zambia. Under increasing pressure to expand the constitutional role of the black majority, white Southern Rhodesians responded by tightening their grip on the government. With the name Northern Rhodesia removed from the map, they renamed their country Rhodesia. On November 11, 1965, Prime Minister Ian Smith declared Rhodesia independent.

The struggle for African majority rule in Rhodesia was fought at two interrelated levels. As in other colonies, nationalist leaders had to persuade Britain to accept their demand for independence and to recognize them as legitimate leaders. In Rhodesia, however, they also had to overcome a solidly entrenched local government that refused to recognize either British imperial authority or the principle of majority rule.

This unique combination of challenges generated one of Africa's most complex and prolonged nationalist struggles. Rivalries among nationalist leaders became as important as the more clearly defined conflicts between them and the white Rhodesian regime. The African who eventually led Zimbabwe to independence was one who remained in the background throughout much of the struggle.

Zimbabwe's first prime minister, Robert Gabriel Mugabe, came into the world at an ominous time in Africa's history. The son of a village carpenter, he was born in Kutama, a Roman Catholic mission station about 50 miles west of Salisbury (now Harare). The date was February 21, 1924 —only five months after Britain granted self-rule to the settlers, who were at that moment organizing their first Legislative Assembly. Mugabe grew up in a society in which white power and white privilege were to be taken for granted, and in which Africans could expect no real political future.

Mugabe spent much of his youth close to Roman Catholic missions and remained a devout Catholic throughout his life. Possessing a passion for learning, he eventually became one of Africa's best-educated leaders. Not surprisingly, he began his career as a teacher. After qualifying at Kutama, he began teaching there when he was only 18. Over the next eight years, he taught at a variety of schools, including Dadaya, a Protestant mission station.

Mugabe was a member of the Shona people, who comprise about three-quarters of Zimbabwe's population. Their history goes back more than a thousand years and encompasses such achievements as the building of Great Zimbabwe (whose ruins gave the modern country its name). However, the Shona began thinking of themselves as a single people only in the 19th century, as alien invasions began pulling them closer together. During the 1840s South Africa's Ndebele kingdom migrated into southwestern Zimbabwe, where it became the dominant regional power. The Ndebele conquered many Shona communities and preyed on others, initiating a legacy of ethnic hostility that endured through their common resistance to the British invasion in the 1890s. Indeed, it persisted into the modern nationalist movement.

Since the Shona outnumber the Ndebele by three to one, Shona-supported political parties have naturally tended to be more powerful. This ethnic cleavage also has a geographical dimension; most Ndebele live in the southwestern region called Matabeleland, and most Shona live in the eastern and northern regions collectively known as Mashonaland. Mugabe did most of his early teaching in Shona areas, but also taught at schools in Ndebele territory.

In 1951 Mugabe spent a year at South Africa's Fort Hare University College, where he completed the first of the several bachelor's degrees that he would earn. There he made his first contacts with Africans from other countries. After returning home to teach at a Roman Catholic school in Umvuma, he began a three-year teaching stint in Northern Rhodesia in 1955. It was an exciting time for him, as Africans in the north were then beginning to enjoy political rights denied to Africans in Southern Rhodesia.

In 1958 Mugabe entered an even more heady political environment: the West African nation of Ghana, which Kwame Nkrumah had led to independence the year before. There he taught at a Roman Catholic teacher-training school in Takoradi. In May 1960 he came home to introduce his new Ghanaian wife, Sarah Francesca Hayfron, to his family; he found Southern Rhodesia's changing political climate so promising that he decided to stay. After living in African-ruled Ghana he hoped to help lead his own country to independence under African rule and made politics his full-time occupation.

Membership in the Central African Federation had helped force Southern Rhodesia's government to grant Africans new political rights. In early 1960 Britain called a conference in London to draft a new constitution for the colony. Africans responded by organizing the National Democratic Party (NDP) to represent them there. Mugabe joined the party and became its publicity secretary under the veteran nationalist leader Joshua Nkomo (an Ndebele). Nkomo and other NDP leaders were willing to accept the new constitution that came out of the London conference, but Mugabe opposed it because he believed it offered limited political power to Africans. His uncompromising position prevailed. At the end of 1961 the government banned the NDP and tightened its laws on political activity.

NDP's former leaders quickly founded the Zimbabwe African People's Union (ZAPU), again with Nkomo as chairman and Mugabe as publicity secretary. After ZAPU led a boycott of the federation elections the following spring, it too was banned, and Mugabe was arrested for his political activities. In 1963 he escaped to Tanganyika, where a split in ZAPU leadership developed. He then returned to Southern Rhodesia and helped found the Zimbabwe African National Union (ZANU), under the leadership of Ndabaningi Sithole. In August 1964 ZANU, too, was banned and Mugabe was among those arrested for engaging in outlawed political activity.

Mugabe's new detention lasted 10 years, moving him through a dreary succession of prisons and camps, but he used his time productively. Through correspondence courses he earned several more college degrees, including a law degree, and tutored fellow prisoners. Meanwhile, significant changes were occurring in the country. In late 1965 the government's new hard-line ruling party, the Rhodesian Front, issued its Unilateral Declaration of Independence (UDI). By casting off Rhodesia's ties to the British Empire, the government hoped to chart its own way in dealing with its African population. Its confident prime minister, Ian Smith, predicted it would be a thousand years before Africans came to power.

While most of the world condemned UDI's obvious design to subvert African rights, Britain took no military action to end Rhodesia's rebellion. Over the next 15 years British leaders periodically tried to negotiate a settlement with the illegal regime while promoting international economic sanctions against Rhodesia. Sanctions strained the landlocked country, but with the help of friendly regimes in South Africa and Portuguese-ruled Mozambique, Rhodesia diversified its economy to compensate for trade restrictions.

In 1972 a British commission visited Rhodesia to study African opinion about a settlement agreement designed to recognize Rhodesia's independence in return for guaranteed progress toward African rule. It found that Africans overwhelmingly opposed the settlement; more importantly, the visit gave the nationalist movement a fresh impetus by forcing the government to permit freer political activity. At the same time, bands of guerrilla fighters began to penetrate white farming areas, and these actions grew into a full-scale African nationalist war against the government. As the war developed, the government gradually realized that it had to make significant political concessions to Africans and began talking with such leaders as Nkomo, Sithole, and Methodist bishop Abel Muzorewa, who had formed the African National Council (ANC) during the British commission's visit.

By late 1974 Smith's government was ready to negotiate a new constitution with African leaders. As a first step, the authorities declared a general amnesty and released all political prisoners, including Mugabe. In December Mugabe joined the leaders who agreed that Muzorewa's ANC would represent all the groups in the upcoming constitutional talks.

Meanwhile, the overthrow of Portugal's right-wing government in early 1974 radically altered the power balance in Southern Africa by setting Angola and Mozambique on speedy paths to independence. Mozambique's abrupt transition to African rule in mid-1975 not only removed a key Rhodesian ally; it prompted South Africa to join the countries urging Rhodesia to negotiate, and it gave nationalist forces safe havens from which to operate against Rhodesia.

These changes helped push Mugabe to the forefront of Rhodesia's liberation struggle. Leaders within ZANU—especially those in its military wing, the Zimbabwe African National Liberation Army (ZANLA)—had been growing dissatisfied with Sithole's moderate leadership. In Mugabe they saw a tough leader unwilling to compromise with the white power structure. He believed that real change would come only if Africans had military strength and were willing to fight. Even before he was released from prison, ZANU leaders secretly made him their top leader. When Sithole joined the nationalist leaders who entered new negotiations with Smith in 1975, there was such confusion among ZANU and ZANLA members about who was in charge that their military operations virtually ceased. By the end of the year, however, most ZANLA leaders recognized Mugabe as their spokesman.

Mugabe, meanwhile, went to Mozambique to help lead ZANU military operations. Over the next four years, as the liberation movement's military effectiveness increased, the government offered more political concessions, but little real progress was made in formal negotiations.

In 1976 Mugabe and Nkomo linked ZANU and ZAPU under the new banner of the Patriotic Front (PF), as they prepared for a negotiating session at Geneva, Switzerland. For the first time Mugabe himself participated in talks with the Smith regime; however, the conference quickly collapsed. The following year Mugabe's leadership position was further strengthened when he was formally elected head of ZANU, and the Organization of African Unity endorsed the PF as the sole representative of the people of Zimbabwe. In early 1978 Mugabe participated in yet another conference, held under American auspices, at Malta. It, too, failed, but Rhodesia lifted its ban on ZANU and other parties in May.

Frustrated by repeated failures in negotiations with the PF, Smith's government initiated its own settlement by bringing Muzorewa, Sithole, and other Africans into the government. With Muzorewa as prime minister of a renamed "Zimbabwe Rhodesia," the new arrangement gave the appearance of African majority rule. However, Mugabe and others operating outside of the country refused to recognize the new government and continued the war. Mugabe's refusal, once again, to compromise helped bring about one of the most remarkable political turnarounds in modern world history. In September 1979 he led a delegation to London for a decisive round of talks: this time Rhodesia voluntarily renounced its independence and agreed to the restoration of British colonial rule.

In January 1980 Mugabe returned to Rhodesia to participate in the country's first all-race elections. In a surprise move, he broke from Nkomo to run a slate of candidates under his original party, now called ZANU-PF. After his party won a strong majority in the late February general elections, the new British governor, Lord Soames, invited Mugabe to form a government. On April 18, 1980, the country officially became independent as Zimbabwe, with Mugabe its first prime minister.

Zimbabwe's independence was a notable achievement after an unusually prolonged and bitter struggle, but it did not solve all the country's problems. Decades of political rivalries and violence left a legacy of bitterness and enmity. Moreover, the intensity of the liberation struggle had raised the expectations of the generally impoverished African majority, and it would be impossible to quickly satisfy all their demands.

Compared to other tropical African countries, Zimbabwe began its independence with a relatively developed economy. It had an exceptionally productive agricultural sector that made it one of the few African countries capable of exporting food. However, it was handicapped by a staggering unemployment rate, and its rural population clamored for fertile land—most of which was owned by a few thousand white families. Mugabe professed to be a Marxist committed to socialism but had to accept the reality that Zimbabwe had an efficient capitalist economy dependent on Europeans.

Dependence on Europeans must have particularly galled him. The independence constitution contained a clause guaranteeing Europeans disproportionate representation in parliament, and Mugabe had accepted this to avoid the economic chaos that would result from a headlong flight of Europeans. As prime minister, he adopted a conciliatory stance and did little more than talk about the need for Socialist revolution. Eventually, about two-thirds of the Europeans left Zimbabwe, but most white farmers stayed and remained bulwarks of the agricultural sector in the late 1990s.

Mugabe's relationship with Joshua Nkomo and the Ndebele-dominated ZAPU proved more troublesome. ZANU-PF's sweeping electoral victory put Mugabe in full control of the government, permitting him to appoint or dismiss ZAPU members to his cabinet at his discretion. Through the first seven years of independence he had an on-again, off-again alliance with Nkomo that was apparently resolved in 1987 when they signed the Unity Pact. Under this agreement ZANU-PF absorbed ZAPU, and Mugabe made Nkomo one of the nation's two vice presidents, at the same time a new constitution transformed Mugabe's office into an executive presidency at the end of the year.

Meanwhile, the new nation faced the problem of managing the various military forces, which consisted of government troops, ZANLA, and ZAPU's military wing, the Zimbabwe People's Revolutionary Army (ZIPRA). Many former freedom fighters were absorbed in the rebuilt national army, but many others remained at large. The government considered the loyalty of ZIPRA troops to be suspect, and reports of serious battles between them and government troops came out of Matabeleland in the early 1980s. Even more ominous were little-publicized reports of large-scale

In May 1997 President Mugabe (right) greeted South African president Nelson Mandela when the latter came to Harare to open a forum on Southern African business and economic issues. (Reuters/Howard Burditt/Archive Photos)

Our culture and
traditions allow for
only one leader.
Mugabe is our king.
Why should he have to
run for election?
Britain's queen does
not run for election.

—Didymus Mutasa

atrocities against Ndebele civilians committed by North Korean–trained government soldiers. The Catholic Commission for Peace and Justice published a full report on these atrocities in early 1997, presenting strong evidence that if Mugabe himself had not been responsible for the massacres, he had at least been aware of them.

As Mugabe's tenure in office continued, he increasingly assumed dictatorial powers. As early as February 1981 his government took control of the country's major newspapers and later took over the major broadcast media. Domination of the country's news media let Mugabe manipulate the news, but he could not control it completely. While his personal integrity was rarely questioned, top-ranking members of his government were involved in scandals that might have brought down governments in Western democracies. Nevertheless, through the presidential election of 1996, he faced no serious electoral challenges. By then, however, he was coming more under attack for certain personal excesses and for his government's failure to bring about economic change. He was accused of spending too much time—and money—traveling abroad, while ignoring problems at home, and critics charged that he had created a bloated and inefficient civil service and an oversized cabinet (with 56 members) that were draining 40 percent of the government's budget.

On his 73rd birthday in early 1997 Mugabe had the government stage an opulent birthday party in his honor in an evident attempt to build a personality cult around the event—the "21st February Movement." While candles blazed on a magnificent birthday cake, the revolutionary fire that had blazed during Mugabe's long and successful struggle for liberation appeared to be burning out.

Chronology

February 21, 1924	Robert Mugabe is born at Kutama Mission in Southern Rhodesia's Makonde District
1941–50	teaches at mission schools
1951	graduates from South Africa's Fort Hare University College
1955–58	teaches in Northern Rhodesia
1958–60	teaches in independent Ghana; marries Sarah Francesca Hayfron
1960	returns to Southern Rhodesia; enters full-time politics
1963	goes to Tanganyika; helps found Zimbabwe African National Union (ZANU)
1964–74	is held in various prisons and detention camps after ZANU is banned
1965	Rhodesia Front issues Unilateral Declaration of Independence
1974	Mugabe is released under general amnesty
1975	goes into exile in Mozambique
1976	forms Patriotic Front with Joshua Nkomo
1977	is elected head of ZANU
1978	participates in talks with government and U.S. representatives at Malta

1979	leads ZANU delegation to London conference; Abel Muzorewa is prime minister in Zimbabwe Rhodesia transitional government
1980	Mugabe returns to Zimbabwe for independence elections, which ZANU wins; is sworn in as prime minister of independent Zimbabwe
1984	renews pledge to create a one-party state at ZANU party congress and is reelected head of the party
1985	ZANU wins national election
1987	Mugabe signs Unity Pact with Nkomo, amalgamating ZANU and ZAPU; is inaugurated Zimbabwe's first executive president
1990	wins first presidential election; abandons plan for one-party state
1996	wins reelection against token opposition
1997	faces growing criticisms for excessive government spending on his large cabinet, foreign travel, and personal activities

Further Reading

Cary, Robert, and Diana Mitchell. *African Nationalist Leaders in Rhodesia: Who's Who*. London: Rex Collings, 1977. Biographies of leading figures in Zimbabwe's nationalist movement.

Eide, Lorraine. *Robert Mugabe*. New York: Chelsea House, 1989. Biography in Chelsea's series on world leaders for young adult readers.

Rasmussen, R. Kent, and Steven C. Rubert. *Historical Dictionary of Zimbabwe*. 2d ed. Metuchen, N.J.: Scarecrow Press, 1990. Comprehensive reference work with entries on Mugabe and related subjects.

Smith, David, and Colin Simpson. *Mugabe*. Salisbury, Zimbabwe: Pioneer Head, 1981. First full-length biography of Mugabe.

Worth, Richard. *Robert Mugabe of Zimbabwe*. New York: Julian Messner, 1990. Sympathetic biography in a series for young readers.

Nelson Mandela casting his ballot in the first fully democratic South African election in 1994 (Reuters/Phillipe Wojazer/Archive Photos)

Nelson Mandela of South Africa

F ebruary 1990 was an exciting month in Africa. Namibia, the continent's last colony, was preparing for its independence—a moment that many had thought would never come. Only four decades earlier all but a few African countries had been colonies. The possibility that many more would become free seemed remote. No one had expected to live long enough to see *all* of Africa independent. Yet that day was now at hand.

One person who never expected to see that day was an aging black prisoner in South Africa. When he had entered prison nearly three decades earlier, his country had been ruled by whites, and no black person could even vote. Since then dozens of other African countries had become independent, and scores of black rulers had come and gone, but in South Africa black people *still* could not vote in 1990.

All that was about to change, however. On February 11, 71-year-old Nelson Mandela walked out of prison a free man. Four years later he was president of South Africa.

Nelson Mandela become president of South Africa in 1994, but was born only a year after U.S. president John F. Kennedy and six months after Egyptian president Gamal Abdel Nasser—both of whom made their marks on history and died a generation before Mandela was even out of prison. His political career also differs markedly from those of other African nations' leaders. Unlike most of them, he was not born in a colony developing under the watchful eye of a European imperial power. In 1918 South Africa was already independent in all but name and was on the road to becoming a powerful, industrialized nation. However, it was a nation in which political power was monopolized by whites, who thought they had as much claim to the land as their much more numerous black neighbors.

In the 19th century the political map of South Africa was a patchwork of British colonies and protectorates; republics created by descendants of early Dutch settlers known as Afrikaners; and independent African societies. By the end of the century, however, all the African societies had fallen under British or Afrikaner rule. At the beginning of the 20th century Britain conquered the Afrikaner republics and brought the entire region under its control for the first time. A few years later, however, it decided to unload its responsibility for South Africa.

In 1910 the region was consolidated under a strong unitary government in the new Union of South Africa. Although black Africans outnumbered whites by more than five to one, they had no voice in creating the Union. Many of them, however, were aware of the changes taking place and the dangers involved in Britain's transfer of power to local whites. In 1912 Western-educated African leaders founded a political organization to represent the interests of all black South Africans—the South African Native National Congress (later called the African National Congress, or ANC).

Dedicated to peaceful constitutional change through legal means, ANC leaders struggled valiantly for decades to persuade the white government to acknowledge African political rights. But instead of winning concessions, they could do little more than observe the steady erosion of African political rights. At the same time, Africans suffered economically as Europeans appropriated their land and enacted laws designed to ensure that they would remain a source of cheap labor.

Into this political environment Rolihlahla Mandela was born on July 18, 1918. His birthplace was a tiny rural village near Umtata, the capital of the Transkei district of the eastern Cape Province. His people, the Thembu, were a branch of the Xhosa, distant cousins of the Zulu to the north. Not brought under British rule until the late 19th century, most Thembu still lived under their traditional state system, but their chiefs now ruled under the supervision of European magistrates.

Mandela's mother, Nosekeni Fanny, was the third of the four wives of Gadla Henry Mphakanyiswa, a hereditary chief and councillor to the Thembu king. Mandela himself was thus a member of the Thembu royal family, in line to inherit his father's offices. When he was an infant, his father got into a dispute with a white magistrate that cost him his position and much of his wealth. Afterward, Mandela moved with his mother to the village of Qunu. Though he could see his father only occasionally, Mandela had an idyllic boyhood at Qunu. He tended livestock, played and fought with other boys, and was largely unaware of the outside world.

After Mandela's mother converted to Christianity, he was baptized in the Methodist Church. When he was seven his parents sent him to a Methodist mission school, where his first teacher (an African woman) gave him his English name, Nelson. Two years later his father died and his life changed dramatically. His uncle Jongintaba Dalindyebo, the acting Thembu regent, offered to be his guardian—a suggestion his mother could not refuse. At Jongintaba's village of Mqhekezweni Mandela enjoyed the same privileges and had the same responsibilities as Jongintaba's own children and had every reason to expect that one day he would be a councillor to Thembu kings himself.

Through these years Mandela assisted his uncle in official tasks and admired Jongintaba's masterful leadership at public meetings. In later years Mandela said that he based his own leadership style on what he learned from his uncle: listening carefully to others before expressing his own opinions and working to achieve consensus.

To help groom Mandela for leadership, Jongintaba sent him to good Methodist secondary schools, where he had his first meaningful contacts with non-Xhosa people. As his horizons widened, he began seeing himself as an African, not merely a Thembu. In 1939 he entered the University College of Fort Hare, the only institution of higher learning open to Africans in the entire country. There he flourished academically and took up boxing and running. His political views were conservative, but in his second year he got into trouble by taking a rigid stand on an ethical principle during a student strike. The head of the college warned him that if he did not back down he would be expelled but gave him until the next term to make his decision.

Mandela returned home to Mqhekezweni pondering his future. His uncle bluntly ordered him to obey his principal and return to Fort Hare but then presented him with another situation that drove his college problem out of his mind. Jongintaba had arranged marriages for Mandela and his own son, Justice Dalindyebo. According to Thembu custom, he had every right to make such arrangements, but Mandela and his cousin had become too Western in their thinking to accept brides chosen by someone else. They ran off together to Johannesburg.

In Johannesburg Mandela took a job as a policeman in one of the city's vast underground gold mines. He was soon liberated from that harsh environment, however, when a friend found him a clerking job in a city law office. While working there he completed his bachelor's degree through correspondence courses and began working for a law degree at the University of Witwatersrand. Meanwhile, he came to an understanding with his uncle that allowed him to stay in Johannesburg and marry a woman of his own choosing. In 1944 he married Evelyn Ntoko Mase, who bore him four children (one of whom died in infancy).

Until then Mandela enjoyed a privileged life for an African. However, he also had experienced enough day-to-day indignities from whites and learned enough about racial injustice in his country to understand that there was something fundamentally wrong with the political system. He also believed that he could help change things. After a year or two in Johannesburg he joined the ANC.

Notable more for its endurance than its effectiveness, the ANC had achieved little during its three decades of existence. Mandela soon sided with other young ANC members who had grown impatient with the organization's conservative leadership and wanted more militant action. In 1944 he helped launch the ANC Youth League. His comrades included Walter Sisulu and Oliver Tambo, both of whom became lifelong associates and friends.

As Mandela devoted more time to political activity, his work habits and energy so impressed fellow Youth League members that they elected him league secretary in 1947. His leadership helped the league exercise a growing influence on the ANC's central directorate, to which he himself was later elected.

Meanwhile, 1948 was proving to be a major turning point in South African history. That year's elections brought to power the National Party, which was dominated by Afrikaners, who were the majority of the country's all-white electorate. The party had pledged to protect whites from being swamped by Africans and began to restrict African freedoms with a new policy called apartheid (apartness). Apartheid gradually controlled almost every aspect of race relations through scores of laws that baldly defined Africans as inferior citizens and took away their rights. As the winds of change spread freedom through the rest of the continent, South Africa was busy inventing new ways to make Africans unfree.

The National Party's rise to power lent a new urgency to ANC activities. Mandela helped draw up a program for boycotts, strikes, and various forms of civil disobedience and noncooperation to challenge the new government. Gradually, the entire ANC grew more militant, demanding for Africans direct parliamentary representation, improved education, full trade union rights, and a fairer share of land.

Mandela's national political career began in earnest in 1952, when he organized the ANC's national Defiance Campaign. He urged Africans to refuse to comply with unjust laws, such as passbook rules and curfews that did not apply to whites. The campaign lasted only a few months, but provoked the government to crack down on the ANC and other political and labor organizations. Mandela was among the leaders arrested for "furthering the aims of communism." Although acquitted, he was hit with a "banning" order—which meant he could not participate in ANC activities. By this time he had been elected president of the ANC's Transvaal branch and was deputy to the ANC's new national president, Albert Luthuli. That same year he also qualified as an attorney and set up the country's first black law office with Oliver Tambo in Johannesburg.

Although Mandela was banned from political activity through most of the following decade, he continued to help direct the ANC through messengers he sent to meetings and by occasionally attending meetings in disguise. In late 1956 he was among 156 black, Asian, and white South Africans charged with treason for political activity. There followed an extraordinarily prolonged legal action. As the "treason trial" developed, charges against most defendants were dropped. The courtroom proceedings finally opened in August 1958 and did not end until March 1961. Mandela and Sisulu were among the 30 defendants still under indictment when a judge finally declared them all not guilty.

Before the trial began Mandela had divorced his first wife because she opposed his political activity. In 1958 he married a younger woman, a social worker named Nomzano Winnie Madikizela. Winnie would give him two more daughters and be one of his closest political allies through the difficult years that followed.

Several months after the treason trial ended, the government undertook a constitutional change that posed new threats to African rights by declaring South Africa a republic. As ANC leaders had often done before, Mandela wrote to the prime minister to express his concern about the impact of the change on Africans, but was ignored. To protest the government's action, he helped lead a nationwide stay-at-home strike.

After reluctantly concluding that peaceful change might be impossible in South Africa, Mandela helped establish a paramilitary wing of the ANC called Umkhonto we Sizwe (Spear of the Nation). He was not yet ready to direct violence against fellow human beings, so he had Umkhonto launch a sabotage campaign in late 1961 against power plants, telephone lines, and other facilities that could be destroyed without loss of life. Meanwhile, Mandela himself went underground. Using disguises and traveling at night, he moved about the entire country, speaking to small groups and recruiting new ANC volunteers. His success in evading arrest earned him the nickname "Black Pimpernel"—a takeoff on the fictional "Scarlet Pimpernel" of the French Revolution. More than once he narrowly escaped capture. On one occasion he climbed from a second-story window as the police came through the front door.

In early 1962 Mandela slipped out of South Africa and became, for the first time ever, a free man. While traveling abroad he addressed an international conference in Ethiopia and made arrangements in other African countries for training Umkhonto members. The publicity he received abroad enhanced his international reputation, while infuriating the South African government. When he returned home in the middle of the year, he was quickly arrested and charged with sabotage.

Mandela defended himself in the trial that followed, using the courtroom as a public platform to state that he did not consider himself legally or morally bound to obey laws made by a parliament in which he had no representation. The government lacked evidence that connected him with sabotage, but convicted him of "incitement" of a workers' strike and leaving the country without a passport. In November 1962 he was sentenced to five years at hard labor and sent to the maximum security prison on Robben Island.

The following June police arrested Walter Sisulu and others at the Umkhonto headquarters at a farm called Rivonia, where they found evidence connecting Mandela with sabotage. Mandela was then taken from his prison to Pretoria, where he and the others were again put on trial for sabotage, conspiracy, furthering the aims of communism, and other offenses.

The defendants were determined to use the proceedings, which became known as the Rivonia Trial, as a political forum. They did not deny they had tried to bring down the government. When Mandela testified in April 1964 he delivered a four-hour oration on the history of government repression and ANC efforts to bring about political change peaceably. As Mandela anticipated, the judge ruled him, Sisulu, and six others guilty on all counts. The defendants expected to be sentenced to death; even so, they agreed not to appeal the sentence, which would serve to bolster the political point they wished to make. However, the judge sentenced them to life in prison. Mandela was returned to Robben Island to resume a confinement that would last until 1990.

Of the 27 years that Mandela served in prison, he spent the first 18 on Robben Island, situated in the chilly South Atlantic off of Cape Town. Physical conditions in the prison were severe. For many years Mandela was confined to a cell so small that he could barely stretch out straight on the pad provided for his bedding on the cold concrete floor. Condemned to hard labor, he spent 13 years working in a limestone quarry, whose dust permanently damaged his eyesight, and he collected seaweed in the frigid surf for use in fertilizers.

Communications between prisoners and the outside world were severely restricted. Mandela was permitted occasional visitors, but only for a few minutes at a time, and their conversations were monitored to prevent political discussion. When Winnie visited, Mandela was not even allowed to touch her. His mother died in 1968, but he could not attend her funeral.

Mandela had an exceptional ability to maintain his composure under the most difficult circumstances, as evidenced by the fact that he wrote examination papers for a University of London law course shortly before the conclusion of the Rivonia Trial, even though he expected to be sentenced to die. After several years on Robben Island, he was permitted to resume his legal studies but was hampered by a lack of current textbooks. He also used his time to study other subjects, including the Afrikaans language, which he wanted to learn in order to understand his oppressors. For several years he lost his study privileges after warders claimed to find evidence he was keeping an illegal journal.

Relentless pressure on the South African government from both inside and outside the country gradually improved conditions for Mandela and other prisoners. Nevertheless, his imprisonment seriously eroded his health, even though he maintained a vigorous exercise regimen. Despite the terrible rigors of his confinement, mistreatment by warders, loneliness and isolation, he managed to maintain a sense of humor and hope for the future.

Even in the grimmest times in prison . . . I would see a glimmer of humanity in one of the guards, perhaps just for a second, but it was enough to reassure me and keep me going. Man's goodness is a flame that can be hidden but never extinguished.

—Nelson Mandela

During Mandela's early years of confinement prisoners were not allowed to gather or talk with each other. Later these restrictions were relaxed, and Mandela talked politics with fellow prisoners whenever he could and organized study groups. During the 1970s political protests increased throughout South Africa, particularly after June 1976, when police in Soweto killed more than 100 African students who were peacefully protesting having to learn Afrikaans in their schools. Increased arrests brought younger political prisoners to Robben Island, giving Mandela the chance to bridge the gap between the generations. His influence on the younger prisoners was such that Robben Island become known to many as "Mandela University."

International efforts to get Mandela out of prison accelerated in 1980 after a black South African newspaper published a banner headline calling for his release. The United Nations added its voice to the Free Mandela Campaign with a Security Council resolution demanding that South Africa free all its political prisoners. In response, the government improved prison conditions somewhat; it allowed political prisoners to receive newspapers and released Mandela from working in the lime quarry. Two years later, without advance warning, the government suddenly moved Mandela, Sisulu, and three other prisoners to Pollsmoor, a modern prison south of central Cape Town. Pollsmoor offered the prisoners a better climate and more physical comforts, but Mandela and his comrades were confined to a single spacious cell isolated from all other prisoners.

Through the 1980s world pressure on South Africa to abandon its apartheid policies and democratize its government mounted, along with violent antigovernment protests within the country. Private individuals, organizations, and governments around the world denounced the South African regime in increasingly harsh terms. Even more important, many businesses voluntarily withdrew their investments from South Africa and foreign governments—including the United States—enacted economic sanctions restricting their citizens' investments in and trade with South Africa. Reduced investments, lost foreign markets, and rising import prices eventually cost South Africa's economy well over 100 billion dollars. Between growing damage to the economy and rising levels of domestic political violence, it was becoming ever harder for the government to resist political change.

Demands to release Mandela and all the other political prisoners became inextricably connected with demands for radical political change. As a symbol of South African repression, Mandela was becoming a more powerful opponent of the government from inside prison than he would have been as a free man. Though he was offered several chances to be released, he regarded his own freedom as identical to that of the nation as a whole and refused to compromise his principles merely to improve his own situation.

During the mid-1980s Prime Minister P. W. Botha became more willing to deal with African leaders and hoped to lessen pressure on his government by finding an acceptable way to release Mandela. By then Mandela had serious health problems and the government feared he might die in prison and become even more dangerous as a martyr. In 1985 Botha publicly offered Mandela his release if he would renounce violence as a political weapon. In a reply his daughter Zinzi read to a rally at Soweto's football stadium, Mandela refused to accept *any* conditions for his release; he instead invited Botha himself to renounce violence.

After Mandela was diagnosed as having tuberculosis in 1988, he was moved to a cottage at Victor Verster Prison, 30 miles from Cape Town. In July 1989 Botha (whose title was now executive president), met with Mandela personally. Three months later the government began releasing Sisulu and other political prisoners. Events started moving even faster after Frederik W. de Klerk replaced Botha as president toward the end of the year. In December de Klerk met with Mandela. Then, in February 1990, he startled the world by announcing in parliament that he would lift the ban on the ANC and 60 other groups and release Mandela without conditions. Meanwhile, the government began rescinding the apartheid laws of the previous four decades.

On February 11 Nelson Mandela walked out of Victor Verster Prison, hand in hand with Winnie. As he rode into Cape Town, his reception—by both black and white South Africans—was tumultuous. Over the next several days he addressed huge crowds throughout South Africa. Several months later he began a trip around the world that included a triumphal tour of the United States, in which he addressed

Nelson and Winnie Mandela wave to supporters as Mandela leaves Victor Verster Prison on February 11, 1990, after 27 years of confinement. (Reuters/ Ulli Michel/Archive Photos)

the U.S. Congress. Meanwhile, the ANC began reconstituting itself as a legal political party and exiled South Africans started coming home from all over the world.

In the months the followed, ANC leaders began preliminary negotiations with the government that would lead to drafting a new constitution. In mid-1991 Mandela was elected president of the ANC, and at the end of the year the Convention for a Democratic South Africa (CODESA) formally opened. A year later Mandela and de Klerk signed a historic agreement approving the arrangements for the free election of a legislature that would draft a new constitution and serve as the country's transitional lawmaking authority.

> The truth is that we are
> not yet free; we have
> merely achieved the
> freedom to be free,
> the right not to be
> oppressed. We have
> not taken the final step
> of our journey,
> but the first step on a
> longer and even more
> difficult road.
>
> —Nelson Mandela

As a result of their agreement, both men shared the Nobel Peace Prize in 1993.

In late April 1994 Mandela voted for the first time in his life as the entire nation turned out for South Africa's first truly democratic national elections. Although political violence had continued to disturb the country after Mandela's release, the elections themselves were remarkably peaceful. As expected, the ANC won a large majority of the new parliament's seats. However, to Mandela's relief, it did not win the two-thirds majority needed to overrule other parties.

On May 9 the new parliament opened. Not only did it have its first ever nonwhite members, it also had more than 100 women after having had only one female member in its previous history. After the legislators were sworn in, Walter Sisulu's wife, Albertina, nominated Mandela for president. Cyril Ramaphosa seconded the motion, and then the parliament elected Mandela unanimously. The following day he was officially inaugurated.

After decades of political violence and unrest, the peacefulness with which South Africa transformed itself from a white-ruled country to a true, multiracial democracy with a black president was remarkable—a change probably without precedent in the history of the world. Much of the credit for this transformation belonged to Mandela, a leader of exceptional moral stature. Mandela did not merely oppose white domination; he opposed domination by any racial group, including Africans. By standing firm in his principles and enduring extraordinary sacrifices that robbed him of most of his adult life, he helped force change, while proving beyond any doubt that he was a leader who could be trusted to keep his word. Without him to lead South Africa through its transition to majority rule, the white government might well have tried to retain power much longer.

The collapse of apartheid and arrival of majority rule did not automatically solve all of South Africa's problems. Mandela worked quickly to instill confidence among the country's whites—who had been raised to believe they would never share power with blacks—but his government still faced enormous challenges. Having the vote for the first time in their lives gave Africans a giddy sense of euphoria, but it alone could not satisfy the expectations that freedom brought. Decades of apartheid had created a huge disparity in white and black income levels. Black South Africans had an unemployment rate of more than 40 percent, millions of Africans lived in homes without electricity or running water, and violent crime was on the increase.

What the future held for South Africa remained uncertain during the first few years of Mandela's presidency. However, few people doubted that he was the best possible person to lead them into that future.

Chronology

July 18, 1918	Nelson Rolihlahla Mandela is born near Umtata, Transkei
1939–40	attends University College of Fort Hare
c. 1943	joins the African National Congress (ANC)

1944	helps found ANC's Youth League; marries Evelyn Ntoko Mase
1952	organizes national Defiance Campaign; starts law partnership with Oliver Tambo
1956	is arrested for treason
1958	marries Nomzano Winnie Madikizela; treason trial begins
1961	Mandela is found not guilty; organizes sabotage campaign
1962	travels outside of South Africa; receives five-year sentence for leaving country illegally and encouraging strikers
1964	is sentenced to life in prison for sabotage
1976	Soweto massacre spurs opposition to apartheid
1980	Free Mandela Campaign begins
1982	Mandela is moved to Pollsmoor Prison
1985	refuses offer of a conditional release
1988	is moved to Victor Verster Prison
1989	meets with presidents P. W. Botha and F. W. de Klerk
1990	de Klerk lifts the ban on the ANC and other political organizations; Mandela is freed without conditions
1991	Convention for a Democratic South Africa opens
1992	Mandela and de Klerk agree on plan for transition to democracy and full rights for Africans
1993	Mandela and de Klerk share Nobel Peace Prize
April 1994	ANC wins large majority in national elections; Mandela is inaugurated president

Further Reading

Benson, Mary. *Nelson Mandela: The Man and the Movement.* Rev. ed. New York: W.W. Norton, 1994. Biography by a South African who committed her own life to the struggle for liberation.

Denenberg, Barry. *Nelson Mandela: "No Easy Walk to Freedom."* New York: Scholastic Books, 1991. Biography for young readers, with considerable background information on South Africa.

Katz, Bobbi. *Meet Nelson Mandela.* New York: Random House, 1995. Brief but reliable biography for young adult readers.

Mandela, Nelson. *The Struggle Is My Life.* Rev. ed. New York: Pathfinder Press, 1986. Collection of Mandela's early speeches and writings.

———. *Long Walk to Freedom.* Boston: Little, Brown, 1994. Engrossing autobiography, which Mandela began writing in 1973 and finished shortly after becoming president.

Meer, Fatima. *Higher than Hope: The Authorized Biography of Nelson Mandela.* New York: Harper & Row, 1988. Full-length biography by a close friend of Mandela's.

Stefoff, Rebecca. *Nelson Mandela: Hero for Democracy.* Rev. ed. New York: Fawcett Columbine, 1994. Biography for young adults.

Index

This index is designed as an aid to access the narrative text and special features. **Boldface** numbers indicate main headings. *Italic* numbers indicate illustrations.